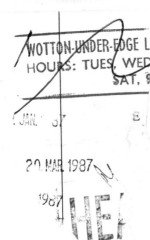

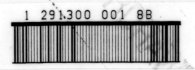

# The
# Wild Garden

*also by Judith Berrisford*

Rhododendrons and Azaleas
Gardening on Lime
The Small Shrub Garden

A *Helleborus* × *orientalis* seedling. All the hellebores are excellent wild garden plants.

# The
# *Wild Garden*

JUDITH BERRISFORD

FABER & FABER
24 Russell Square London

First published in mcmlxvi
by Faber & Faber Limited
24 Russell Square London WC1
Printed in Great Britain by
Latimer Trend & Co Ltd Plymouth

*For*
*Isolene, Nida, Eric, Audrey, Gordon, Molly, Ron,*
*Rose, Robin, Geraint, Liz, Margery, Carrie, Mario,*
*Sophie, Nina and all my gardening friends in North*
*Wales, North Staffordshire, Cornwall and wherever*
*they may be.*

# *Contents*

PART TWO

*Wild Gardener's Plant Dictionary*

# Illustrations

A *Helleborus* × orientalis seedling. All the hellebores are excellent wild garden plants.
*frontispiece*

## *Acknowledgements*

I SHOULD like once again to acknowledge my gratitude to Mr. Richard de la Mare for giving me the chance to write about my favourite subject and to Mr. Lawrence Hills for his helpful and stimulating comments on my drafted scheme for the book; to Mrs. Lamb for deciphering my handwriting and typing the manuscript; to Mr. Graham Thomas for once again making available to me his wonderful selection of photographs of rare and interesting plants; to Mr. J. E. Downward for allowing me to use his splendid colour photograph for the cover and to Miss Phyllis White for her patient co-operation and first-class skill in photographing plants in my own garden and in other gardens in North Wales.

# PART ONE

# CHAPTER ONE

# Wild Gardening
# Today

To most of us the term 'wild garden' evokes a picture of a piece of woodland, a streamside or perhaps an old orchard —an attractive plot of ground which can be made even more delightful by the introduction of suitable plants, native and exotic, which will add to the setting without spoiling it. In such a place the emphasis must always be on the aesthetic. One must take care 'not to startle the nightingales'.

Today opportunities for wild gardening are widened— new bungalows and houses are sometimes built within the boundaries of large old gardens or woodlands or even on heathland or in limestone quarries, offering a chance to keep the planting and setting of the property strictly in character while at the same time reducing the labour involved both in the making of the garden and in its upkeep.

Not everyone has the ideal setting. But within most of us there is a secret longing for a piece of flowering wilderness, however small, in which to make our naturalistic plantings. A planting of three to five birch trees in rough grass will give us a place to enjoy our snowdrops, aconites and Lent lilies; in which we can plant foxgloves and columbines, trilliums and dog's tooth violets; where the musk rose and honeysuckle can run up the trees to give us our own little piece of the wild in miniature—a sweet disorder that may bring us perhaps the happiest moments of our garden lives.

Wild gardening appeals also to those who are too busy to devote much time to their hobby but are faced with the taming of a naked and untouched area of ground around a new property. No one, I must hasten to say, can achieve even a *wild* garden without a certain amount of work but wild gardening does offer the most pleasing returns for the least time and effort spent in maintenance.

Trees, flowering shrubs, including the less formal shrub roses, the more vigorous herbaceous subjects and bulbs are the main planting material in any wild garden and of these only the strongest-growing bulbs will survive without ground preparation. Even the tougher daffodils such as 'John Evelyn' and 'Carlton' and the camassias and Spanish bluebells, if planted in turf, need some control of the grasses if they are not to be choked out of existence. Rough grass in which bulbs are planted must be cut (by scythe or rotoscythe) at least twice a year—in June or later, when the bulb foliage has withered and in late November to make room for the emergent shoots. Where crocuses and the smaller daffodils such as *Narcissus pseudo-narcissus*, the Lent Lily, *N. triandrus albus*, the 'Angel's Tears' narcissi, and the Hoop-Petticoat Daffodil *N. bulbo-codium* and its varieties are grown it helps if the grass is scarified by a rake after the November cut to remove any tufts of dried grass which would otherwise clog the turf. Primroses, violets, cowslips, columbines and the pink-and-blue-crozier-flowered lungworts also need these attentions.

Trees, climbers, shrubs and most herbaceous plants must be planted in weed-free, well-dug soil if they are to get away to a good start. This means that they must each have their individual site, cleared of turf or other growth, dug a couple of spits deep and enriched. Alternatively they need to be set in specially prepared community beds. One cannot just dig a hole in the grass, drop in a plant and expect it to thrive. The roots of the encroaching grass rob it of moisture and food, the blades and stems deprive it of light and air and it dies. Even if a grass-free site can be found in woodland it will probably be so full of roots that nothing could be expected to grow until the old roots have been severed and fresh, enriched soil added to give the plant a start. Once a plant is thoroughly established the competition of other roots does not seem to matter—in fact established plants seem to grow better in company with others. And with taller subjects even encroaching grass seems not to have any adverse effect after the first three or four years. But the first three or four years are vital. Watchful care must be exercised throughout them if the young plants are to get away to a satisfactory start.

Wild gardening, then, is certainly not entirely work-free. It is, however, the most rewarding and satisfying form of gardening I know. Nothing can give more pleasure than a small patch of woodland enhanced by a few choice shrubs and trees, its floor freed of brambles and other harmful growth but dappled with bulbs, while, later, foxgloves stand sentinel beneath the trees and the scent of honeysuckle enriches the air. Or one may have an old orchard with primroses and violets wreathing the boles of the trees, daffodils and narcissi matching the clouds of blossom with drifts and pools of light. To follow, columbine and cornflowers stipple the turf and with hedge parsley embroider a softly coloured pattern on the grass. Downland gardens, too, give pleasure with their stretches of turf enhanced by *Spirea arguta*, the Bridal Wreath, and the single golden flowers of *Kerria japonica simplex* in May are to be succeeded by the burgeoning shrub roses and weigela and *Cornus kousa chinensis* with its startling beauty, until the berberis colour to flame in the autumn

B

and cotoneaster and stranvaesia warm November and December with their fire of berries.

The present age, with its motorways and high-speed roads cutting into the landscape like giant scars, brings opportunities for another kind of wild gardening. Steep roadside banks, dumped soil loads, disused gravel pits, worked out open-cast coal seams, slag-heaps and mine tips—all these disfigurements of twentieth-century Britain may be beautified by the appropriate authorities and planted out with trees and shrubs. Birch and mountain ash, bracken, bluebells and willow herb will thrive on the waste mounds of colliery, slate quarry and lead mine alike, serving not only to mask their ugliness but also to bind and hold the surface. For steep roadside embankments and escarpments, sea-buckthorn, burnet roses (and other creeping species such as *R. nitida* and *paulii*) may be used along with the best berrying forms of snowberry, with berberis, dwarf willows, spreading junipers and double gorse to hold the soil while at the same time forming wild plantings of considerable beauty. Crash-barriers also are needed and these, too, may be made interesting and beautiful by drift-plantings of rose species and suitable shrubs whose growth is pliant and whippy enough yet thick enough to enable them to act as catch-nets and deflectors. The Forestry Commission also has its opportunities to enliven its somewhat sombre plantations particularly where they abut on to well-used roads and footpaths. In North Wales this has in places been imaginatively done with an eye to autumn colour but there is a need for year-round interest which could so easily be added. These exciting challenges as well as the prospects and possibilities for individual makers of wild gardens will be dealt with later in the book.

CHAPTER TWO

# The Wild Wood

THERE can be few true gardeners who at some time or another have not toyed with the idea of a piece of woodland and been beguiled by the thought of making a wild garden therein. It sounds so delightful, the mossy woodland floor, the dappled shade, the clumps of lilies and the choice rhododendrons, their scarlet, apricot or primrose trumpets gleaming through the shade. Or one's vision may be simpler than this. Perhaps one would go no further than the planting of bluebells and wild orchis—the introduction of primroses and wood anemones. Whatever the ideal it is much less easy of achievement than one might hope. Gardening in a wood in the initial stages at any rate is a constant battle against the wild.

In the winter when most of the branches are leafless and the dark greens of ivy, holly and yew are the only solid furnishings, the woodland seems remarkably bare. The soft leaf-mould underfoot invites one to plant one's treasures. For the first spring all may be well; the snowdrops may droop their green-tipped bells endearingly above the ivy; the daffodils will nod their golden trumpets; the bluebells make their wood-smoke haze. Yet come high summer and all is lost beneath the choking tangle of bramble and goose-grass, dog's mercury, ground elder, jungles of unflowered honeysuckle and tussocks of grass.

The amount of undergrowth varies of course from wood to wood. Under the dark canopy and between the stilt-like stems of spruce and fir only a few brambles and ferns appear above the carpet of fallen pine needles. But here it is too dark and airless for anything else to grow. Much felling and clearance would be needed before one could hope to wild garden at all. The nearer one comes to the ideal conditions of well-spaced oaks or birches with their light leaf cover above, the greater becomes the tangle beneath. Before one plants, the thickets of bramble must be cleared. Grass must be uprooted from the sites of shrubs and the imported treasures set in mundane beds. Ivy can be left in the areas not to be planted but it should not be allowed to choke the trees. If the thick stems are sawn through at their bases the growth can then be pulled away from the trunks. Bracken presents a more difficult problem. Wearing thick gloves to protect one's fingers from the glass-sharp stems one can pull up the fronds. Some of the rhizomes, however, will inevitably be left. The only real solution lies in cutting down the bracken fern each year as it appears, thus giving no chance for regeneration by spores. The regular removal of the leaves also cuts off the food supply of the plant, thus weakening it until it dies. Three years will usually serve to eradicate bracken by this means. Beds or planting sites, though, must be thoroughly cleared of the rhizomes by digging before planting is carried out.

It might be thought that an easier remedy lies in a brush-wood spray or other weed-killer but although one might use 'paraquat' to weaken bracken on the open hillside I would never use weed-killers in woodland. Not only might they harm the trees but by doing away with ivy, mosses and harmless ferns they destroy the natural cover of the woodland floor and often linger in pockets of soil to affect later plantings. I have known of so many mys-terious plant deaths that have later been traced back to the use of weed-killer that I would recommend them only to deal with vegetable plots or to be used on strictly scheduled lines for the control of weeds between the rows of commercial plantings. In nurseries and on fruit farms and small-holdings the pre-emergence weed-killers play a useful part. Flame-guns, although effecting a temporary improvement by consuming top-growth, leave the deep roots of couch-grass, nettle and brambles untouched. Their use in woodland, moreover, is fraught with the danger of accidental fire.

Often a woodland site will be found to be too crowded to allow for attractive planting. It is necessary then to decide what trees are to be cut down and arrange for them to be felled before planting begins. When having a house or bungalow built on a wooded site it may be possible to come to terms with the builder to arrange for the removal of unwanted trees and for the clearance of scrubby thickets. Otherwise it is usually possible to find a timber merchant who will cut down and remove the surplus without payment in exchange for the timber. Thickets of elder, small trees and scrub can quite readily be uprooted by means of a tree-jack. All branches and timber must be removed or burnt. Timber left lying about rots and becomes a source of disease as well as harbouring wood-lice and other pests. The decision of what trees to cut is often a hard one but it is wise to aim at leaving a variety of growth. Evergreens such as laurel or wild rhododendron should be left on the outskirts as they provide good shelter. Holly, yew, spruce, fir, pine and larch add notes of character among broad-leafed trees. Elms are often victims to disease so where there is felling to be done they should be among the first to be cut. Sycamores are greedy and rather characterless and should not be allowed to predominate. Oak and alder are good. They provide light shade and shelter and mix well with other plantings. Little will grow under beech but well-grown beeches are too noble to be felled. Birches

often grow in a dense scrub which should be thinned
leaving the best specimens to show the full beauty of their
silvery bark. The predominant aims should be to leave
attractive mature specimens wherever possible but to let
in sufficient light to allow the new introductions to grow
freely. At the same time care must be taken not to let in
too much wind.

Woodland gardens are blessed above all on account of
the shelter they provide enabling many beautiful plants to
be grown with less risk of wind and frost damage. Some
woodlands, even on chalk and limestone have a top few
inches, at least, of acid soil in which rhododendrons,
camellias and other lime-senstitive treasures will grow.
Before ordering quantities of expensive plants, however,
it is as well to check by a soil test the exact pH of the
planting sites. From 6·5 downwards is safe for camellias
and for most rhododendrons in woodland conditions.

Year-round interest is of course the aim and a wild garden in woodland can be made to yield treasures for indoor
decoration through every week of the year.

In January one of the brightest pictures may be created
by a planting of the deciduous *Rhododendron mucronulatum*
which carries an airy mass of azalea-like flowers in bright
rose-purple on its bare winter twigs. To combine with it,
the gold-tinselled witch-hazel *Hamamelis mollis* is most
effective and, contrary to oft-stated misconception, the
witch-hazels are not sensitive to lime in the soil. They will
thrive in woodland anywhere. All they need, in common
with all other wild garden subjects, is to be planted in a
well-prepared site with a forkful of rotted stable manure
or a couple of handfuls of hop-manure for encouragement.
Thereafter they must be kept free from choking grass and
weeds for the first few years at any rate. After that the
natural woodland carpet of ivy, periwinkle or violets will
do little harm. Ferns, too near the roots, will rob such
plants of nourishment. Ferns are delightful and right in

a wild setting. They make fine ground cover and prevent the encroachment of weeds but they should not be allowed to grow within the root circle of rhododendrons, witch-hazels, camellias or azaleas. Coarse shrubs such as berberis or cotoneaster will generally be untroubled by the competition.

In addition to *Hamamelis mollis* with its maroon-centred spiders of gold there is a valuable new hybrid between this species and *H. japonica* which is known as 'Jelena' with orange-copper flowers. In autumn, too, this makes a useful contrast as its leaves turn to orange and flame before falling whilst those of *H. mollis* become yellow. *H. japonica arborea* is also useful, though scentless, as flowering later it extends the season to March. The witch-hazels and *Rhododendron mucronulatum* will flower in sun or shade. The scented flowers of the witch-hazel are extremely resistant to frost and last in full beauty for about a month. Those of the rhododendron are more fleeting and are browned by more than three or four degrees of frost. If planted on the north or west of a holly or laurel or under the branch spread of a deciduous tree they are less likely to be damaged. If, however, the first blooms are frosted they will be followed by another crop.

This useful trait of successional blooming is shown too by the more conventional evergreen *R*. 'Nobleanum' which bears globular crimson trusses in mid-winter. There is also *R*. 'Nobleanum Venustum' with flowers of luscious pink, and a white form which is later to bloom.

Delightful in sunny clearings on acid or alkaline soil is the rose-tinted, scented *Viburnum × bodnantense* 'Dawn'. In more shady places the cowslip-fragrant *Mahonia japonica* will shine with its drooping spikes of lemon-flowers above whorls of handsome spiny pinnate leaves.

In the prepared ground beneath such shrubs as these, the easy Lenten roses, hybrids of *H. orientalis* and its affinities will do well. They will not seriously rob the soil and their dark, fingered leaves make handsome ground cover. From late January (and sometimes earlier) to the end of March their drooping bowl-shaped, speckled flowers in greeny-white, apple-blossom, peach, claret and a matt-finished purple that is almost black, will entrance and intrigue. The narrower-fingered *H. foetidus* has smaller flowers of apple-green which become rimmed with wine as they age. These are borne in large clusters. This plant is a British native and I have seen it growing thickly in Welsh limestone woodland and lining the hedge bottom on four sides of a field. Lit by the thin January sunshine the chartreuse cups were a glowingly beautiful sight.

Also native to British woodlands are two of the daphnes, the green-flowered *D. laureola* and the purple *D. mezereum*. Both these are sweetly scented and with the white-flowered form of *mezereum* will seed themselves and colonize to some extent.

Using plants which will make themselves at home and spread in this way is one of the pleasures of wild gardening and by limiting one's weeding to the removal by hand of those weeds which encroach on the actual planting sites one gives the wanted seedlings a chance to establish where indiscriminate hoeing might have destroyed them.

One of the toughest and most reliable of February-blooming shrubs is *Cornus mas*, a member of the dog-wood family which carries tiny thread-like yellow flowers on its bare branches in such profusion as to make the whole plant look as if it were outlined in gold. It has the form of a spreading shrub or gnarled small tree and should be planted either on the outskirts of the wood or in a clearing where the sunlight will catch its branches and light up the flowers.

At about the same time many camellias bloom—some in fact will flower even earlier in sheltered, sunny corners —such are the × *williamsii* cultivars 'Mary Christian' (phlox pink) and 'Hiraethlyn' (palest blush). The double white *Camellia japonica* 'Nobilissima' and the pink *C. japonica* 'Gloire de Nantes' are also early, blooming before the majority which follow at the end of the month and in March. Fine for woodland where their blooms will not be spoiled by the weather are the delicate coloured *C. j.* 'Magnoliaeflora' and the single white 'Alba Simplex'. The warm pink 'Lady Clare' is also delightful and like 'Magnoliaeflora' has a low, sweeping habit which makes it splendid to plant beside a path.

Of the reds the semi-double 'Adolphe Audusson' is one of the finest. It is pure geranium-scarlet in colour and lit by a great boss of golden stamens.

One of the loveliest camellias of all in its best form is the luscious double *C. × williamsii* 'Donation'. 'Salutation' and 'Citation', too, are excellent and advantage should be taken of the opportunities offered by woodland to grow them to perfection.

With expensive plants it need hardly be said that the returning rabbits are a menace to be watched. If possible the wild garden should be netted against them with one-inch mesh sunk for a foot into the ground. Alternatively individual shrubs and trees should be surrounded with wire-netting. As a short-term measure spraying the ground with *Renardine* will be found effective.

Easy rhododendrons that are delightful in woodland in the early spring are *R.* 'Praecox' and its sister seedling 'Emasculum' which flowers a fortnight later and *lutescens* in pinky-mauve and yellow respectively. They have small leaves and attractive azalea-type open flowers and are light and not too dominant in growth. To yield heavy trusses of glorious scarlet *R.* 'Cornubia' is a safe bet in woodland almost anywhere.

At the risk of being accused of a pro-rhododendron bias I must emphasize that rhododendrons in all their forms are wild wood-garden shrubs of the highest value. However, care must be taken not to allow the heavy leafed evergreen hybrids to predominate and room must be left for the lighter growth of the species of the Triflorum series and for the deciduous azaleas.

Among the best and easiest evergreen rhododendrons to choose to flower from April to June are the scarlet, spreading semi-dwarf 'Elizabeth', 'Carita' which opens primrose-champagne from mushroom-pink tinged buds, the scented fawn-pink 'Naomi', cherry coloured 'Winsome', 'Goldsworth Orange', the buff-ochre 'Unique', daffodil yellow Hawk grex 'Crest' or Hawk grex 'Jervis Bay', terra-cotta 'Roman Pottery' of the Fabia grex, and the later 'Tally Ho' in soft true scarlet. The deeper red late 'Gros Claude' or 'Fusilier' and a scented blush, large-growing hybrid of the Fortunei series such as 'Loderi' in one of its many forms to flower in May might also be planted along with the later 'Lodauric' or 'Angelo' to follow.

Of the more lightly built members of the Triflorum series, the near-blue *augustinii* is lovely in association with 'Loderi' or planted beneath the white Japanese cherry 'Shirotae' with its wide spread of snowy blossom. *R. yunnanense* of the same series is pink or pale lavender, speckled with chestnut, and is an extremely hardy and easy rhododendron to grow. With the small, blue-green leaves of the beautiful Cinnabarinum series, the amber *concatenans* and the hybrids of the 'Lady Chamberlain' and 'Lady Rosebery' grexes with their waxen hanging bells are treasures that will succeed easily in the wild wood so long as they are kept free from brambles and other choking growth.

Contrast may be provided by such viburnums as the carnation-scented × *juddii* (a decided improvement on *carlesii*), the even earlier-flowering semi-evergreen × *burkwoodii*, the May-blooming scentless but beautiful *plicatum* var. *tomentosum sterile* with its large snowball flowers and the hydrangea-like lacecap *V.p.* var. *tomen-tosum mariesii*, its branches flattened in an impressively architectural habit of growth. The viburnums will succeed equally well on acid or alkaline soils and flower well even in considerable shade. The chaenomeles (cydonia), how-ever, need a rather more sunny site. Their apple-blossom-shaped flowers in blood-red, orange-scarlet, rose-pink and white last for a long time and are usually followed in autumn by decorative golden 'fruits'. Grown as bushes away from the customary wall they bloom freely but the long spiny growth of midsummer should be pruned off in autumn if the flowers are to be seen to their best advantage.

In May the new Knaphill and Exbury azaleas are colourful and charming as are the older Ghent varieties. For woodland planting I think the yellow shades should predominate as they seem to fit in best with the prevailing green.

The idea of roses in woodland may seem a little incon-gruous at first but there is nothing out of place in the way in which some of the wild species and their near relations make themselves at home. Best of all perhaps is *Rosa moyesii* and its variety 'Geranium'. Their flowers, of blood-red and scarlet respectively, are heraldic in shape and carried on arching canes above one's head in a swirl of fern-like greenery. The flowers in autumn are followed by vivid, carrot-shaped fruit. Also good are the butter-yellow 'Frühlingsgold', the white 'Nevada' and its deep rose-pink sport 'Marguerite Hilling', while *rubrifolia* should certainly be grown for its reddish stems and reddish-tinged, blue-grey, grape-bloom foliage. The climbing species such as the fragrant *moschata*, *longicuspis* and *Sino-wilsonii* with the simpler hybrids like 'Wedding Day' or 'The Garland' may be used with honeysuckle to climb the trees and hang their opulent swags of blossom above one's head.

Happy in woodland where the shade is not too dense

are the more informal of the mock-oranges—'Beauclerk', 'Voie Lactée', 'Belle Etoile' and 'Sybille'—while the deutzias are even more accommodating and will flower well in quite heavy shade. The single-flowered species such as *kalmiaeflora*, *setchuenensis*, and the hybrid 'Magician' are most in keeping with the image of the wild garden.

Also able to endure considerable shade and needing no care other than an occasional glance to ensure that they are free from weed encroachment are some of the tree heaths—*Erica arborea alpina* makes a large bush of bright mossy green, in time reaching four feet or more in height with a considerable spread. Its flowers are an ashy grey in effect and hawthorn scented. They are borne in late April or May. At about this time or a little earlier the rose-purple *E. mediterranea* flowers. Less vigorous, it grows to under three feet in height. Earlier still, flowering at the end of February or early March, *E. mediterranea* 'W. T. Rackliff' is a good plant to come upon in a shady corner with its bright-green close foliage and pure white bells. In more open parts, the winter-flowering, mat-like *E. carnea* varieties are delightful but they are certainly not trouble free. Even when they have spread to form a close carpet they need weeding. Goose-grass, couch and creeping pontentilla are their usual invaders and once they have taken hold are difficult to eradicate. Too shady a place adds to the trouble but these winter heaths should always be clipped over when the flowers are done to ensure close sturdy growth.

A criticism often levelled against wood gardens is that they are so often apt to be dull and rather sombre when the spring and early summer mass of colour from the rhododendrons and azaleas is past. There is absolutely no need for this to happen. Hydrangeas will do extremely well in woodland and flower throughout the summer. Shade and plenty of moisture are their ideal conditions.

Some people say that the mop-headed × *macrophylla*
section is out of place in the wild garden but I really
think this is nonsense. The flower colour of most hydrangeas is blue under woodland conditions and the large bun-
shaped flowerheads in all shades of blue are cool and
attractive under the trees. By all means grow the lacecaps,
too. Their flower-pattern is exquisite and they are extremely valuable but I would never exclude the × *macrophylla* varieties from the wild garden on grounds of taste.
Also effective is *Hydrangea paniculata* with its pyramidal
flower heads that change from green through white to
rose as they age. A bush with flowers in all three stages is
a lovely sight. The tall, baize-leaved 'tree' *H. sargentiana*
makes an effective specimen near the meeting of two
paths or other focal point. Its flowers are individually less
spectacular than those of the ordinary lacecaps but there is
beauty in their misty violet and a grandeur about the whole
plant that makes it worthy of inclusion. *H. villosa*, too, is
good and will keep its blue colour even on limestone.
Perhaps the most individually beautiful of the hydrangeas
are the *serrata* types with fimbriated edges to the petals of
their sterile flowers. Lacecap in type, the flowerheads in
most varieties change to crimson as they age. Of them,
'Grayswood' and 'Rosalba' are usually available from
specialist shrub nurseries. The nearly related *Schizophragma hydrangeoides* is a climbing version of the hydrangea family that is very effective climbing up an oak or
beech or other large tree. Its lacecap flowerheads have a
solitary large bract-like sepal to each non-fertile flower.
Cream in colour, these show up well and the whole plant
has a handsome appearance as it wreathes its way up a tall
tree-trunk.

For July and August where shade is not too dense two
graceful brooms will add colour to the woodland scene.
They are the twelve-foot-high *Genista cinerea* and *G.
aethnensis*. Both yield a drooping shower of scented golden

flowers. In August, too, flower the lovely eucryphias of which the deciduous *E. glutinosa* is the best for the small woodland. Its bowl-shaped white flowers are freckled with tan anthers and its crinkly dark green leaves turn to flame and orange before they fall.

By September, autumn colours are with us in the berries of the native rowan. Some of the leaves of the beech-like parrotia have turned to blood-red and the foliage of the Chinese berberis species and hybrids burns with a fire that matches the scarlet of their globular droplet fruits. From now on the feast of berries builds up. Autumn in the wild wood can be one of the most colourful times of the year. Among the most brilliant displays are those of the crimson-berried *Cotoneaster conspicuus decorus* with its low mounded growth, the taller *C.* 'Cornubia' and the yellow-fruited *C. exburiensis*. Finest of all perhaps is the seldom grown *Berberis vulgaris* with large, elongated brilliant berries and fiery leaves. There is a purple-leaved form, also, of this species which is almost equally good.

As complement to the colours of berries and foliage, the prolific autumn-flowering *Crocus speciosus* may be grown in the shrub beds or in short grass. This crocus is bright hyacinth blue with orange stigmata. It increases well. The colchicums, too, are worth growing. *C. speciosus* and *autumnalis* in its white and mauve forms are the ones to choose along with the named hybrids all of which are good. They are hearty growers and will establish themselves in grass.

Apt to be smothered by tall grasses but quite at home in ivy or in the bare earth at the base of large trees, the tiny wild cyclamen are lovely from autumn to spring. *C. neapolitanum* is the easiest and best for the wild garden. Its shuttlecock flowers are white or pink and its shapely dark green leaves, beautifully silvered, last to form a pleasing background to the snowdrops in spring.

Woodland is the natural home of the common snowdrop, *Galanthus nivalis* and, planted closely in clumps at first, it will soon spread to carpet the ground. Where the snowdrop grows, the winter aconite may or may not thrive. It is worth planting just a few at first to see how they will do in your ground. I have never been successful with *Eranthis hyemalis*. However, where this wildling fails the more robust *E.* × *tubergeniana* will often do well. This hybrid is alleged to set no seed but it does increase vegetatively. Its green-ruffed large golden flowers are borne on sturdy stems and are pretty in association with the snowdrops.

Various daffodils do well in the wood. Perhaps the wild Lent Lily *Narcissus pseudo-narcissus* is the most in keeping with the spirit of the wild garden but so long as they are planted in irregular clumps and drifts of the same variety I think all but the gaudiest new red-cups are permissible. In a damp spot in acid soil, the tiny *N. cyclamineus* will establish itself. This small treasure has a long golden trumpet and a turned-back cyclamen-like perianth giving rise to its specific name. With these small narcissi will associate the early-flowering *Erythronium dens-canis* but this species must have sufficient sunlight to turn back its beautiful flowers.

The North American *Erythronium revolutum* and *E. californicum* need conditions similar to those enjoyed by *Narcissus cyclamineus*. Good hybrids of these species may usually be obtained but unfortunately the species themselves are very rare in Britain. I have been trying unsuccessfully to find a source of supply for the rose-pink *E. revolutum* for several years. All come easily from seed sown *in situ* but take five years to flower.

Lily of the Valley and Solomon's Seal are valuable subjects for wild gardening. Some of the true lilies are easy in woodland conditions. Of these the most likely to establish well and to increase are the August-flowering tall *Lilium*

*henryi* with its orange turkscap flowers, the old-fashion
early yellow *L. pyrenaicum*, the white and purple martag
and the new hybrids 'Destiny' (lemon-yellow) and 'E
chantment' (nasturtium-red). Planted six inches deep
groups of three these will quite rapidly form good clump

Other wild wood subjects are the foxgloves, seed c
which may be purchased in apricot, sulphur or white, t'
North American trilliums ('Wake Robin') with white
corne flowers and the wild geranium species. These,
other herbaceous and bulbous subjects, will be dealt
in the 'Wild Gardener's Plant Dictionary' in the se
part of the book.

Where there is room it may be desirable to create fi
interest by planting an additional tree or two. Flower
cherries are good, particularly the 'November Cher
*Prunus subhirtella autumnalis* which in fact flowers in mi
spells throughout the winter, the spreading blush *yedoensis*
and the splendid whites 'Tai Haku', 'Shirotae' and 'Shimidsui' also the mellow, greeny-yellow 'Ukon'. Laburnums
are best grown as bushes, so that they flower well at eye-
level and illumine the darker places. Magnolias, too, are
ideal as the woodland gives their flowers the protection
they merit. From the small-growing early *stellata* to
*wilsonii* which blooms in June, all are suitable. Worthy of
wider planting are *kobus* with *stellata*-type flowers but
making a small tree, *denudata* with white chalices on bare-
dark-wood, and the wine-purple *liliflora*. For those who
like to look ahead the more recently introduced *sargentiana
robusta* is the tree to plant. Flowering in ten to twelve years
it needs only a third the patience of *campbellii* and its rose-
pink, down-turned, moth-like flowers are the loveliest of
all. Not to be overlooked are the uncommon and pleasing
'Snowdrop Trees'—*Halesia monticola* and *Styrax japonica*
—while for beauty of bark and leaf one must include such
maples as 'Osakazuki'—fiery in autumn—the tatter-
barked *Acer griseum*—which is not however very easy to

1    An ideal setting in which to make a wild garden.

2　Daffodils should be set in cloud-like drifts.

find these days and may have to be raised from seed—the pretty *ginnala* and the snake-bark *A. grosseri* var. *hersii*.

All this may sound ambitious to the wild gardener but there is no need to plant the whole area at once. It is wisest to take in only a small part of the woodland at first —always working in from a path, clearing and consolidating one's plantings and never setting out more plants than one can keep free from weed and bramble. Nor must the exotics form too large a proportion of the scene. Always the native woodland should predominate and any embellishments or additions should be firmly in key with the rest.

CHAPTER THREE

# An Orchard Garden

A FEATURE of the helpful policy of local government under the welfare state has been the monetary grants given
to people to enable them to rebuild old properties, putting
in sanitation and hot-water systems and generally bringing
them up to the standard of modern comfort. This has led
to the conversion of many country cottages—some of
them little more than tumble-down ruins but usually having amid the grass and nettles of an abandoned garden the
apple trees, the pears, plums and damson that the former
cottager relied upon to provide him with fruit, with jams
and jellies almost the year round. It is a pity to grub up
these still productive trees to make the conventional
suburban-type garden that one sadly notices round many
modernized cottages. Far better to be grateful for their
bounty of fruit and blossom, to scythe down and tame the
grassy jungle and find therein the site for that most enjoyable of wild gardens—an orchard garden.

The best wild garden that I have ever had was in such
an orchard. It was quite sixty years old and the trees were
gnarled and shapeless from neglect but still prolific in
fruit. Some inspired person had already begun to make a
wild garden there before we took it over and had most
successfully colonized the grass between the trees with
lungwort—the old-fashioned 'Soldiers and Sailors' or

'Bethlehem Cowslip' of country gardens—*Pulmonaria officinalis*, that lifted its pink-and-blue crozier heads above Disney-like spotted leaves in February—and that in a bleak Midland county.

In March, grape-hyacinths, the large *Muscari* 'Heavenly Blue', flowered along with wild primroses and violets nestling against the boles of the trees. This grape-hyacinth is particularly good for naturalizing. It seeds freely and in grass the straggly leaves that precede and outlast the deep-blue flowers are not noticed.

Daffodils, of course, are perfect beneath the opening pink buds of the apple-blossom. Those that succeed in grass range from the early-blooming *Narcissus obvallaris*, the small 'Tenby Daffodil', to the standard varieties 'Magnificence', 'King Alfred' and 'Carlton'. 'John Evelyn' with its paler perianth and apricot-cup naturalizes well while the white 'Mount Hood' is strong enough to thrive. 'White Nile' is another pale variety that should be planted in drifts. The later-flowering old favourite, the 'Pheasant's Eye' narcissi, though shy to bloom the first season will quickly establish and increase to form fragrant pools of glistening white, round-perianthed flowers under the trees.

Tulips also will naturalize satisfactorily. I have seen the Darwins growing wild in grass and looking very effective. There are those who will shudder at thought of this, I know, because there is perhaps something artificial about the fat globular flowers of these Dutch hybrids that seems out of keeping with the ideal of wild gardening. Yet if one chooses only the white and yellow varieties and leaves them alone to increase year by year they will form larger groups and at the same time the flowers will become smaller until they achieve almost an untamed grace. For those who are too shocked by this idea I can recommend two wild species—the yellow, pointed-petalled *Tulipa sylvestris* and the later geranium-red *T. sprengeri*. This last is expensive to buy nowadays but a dozen bulbs are a good investment as this is a species that will truly naturalize itself, increasing over the years by self-sown seed.

Several herbaceous subjects will carry on the interest from here. In our wild orchard we grew the traditional cottage paeony—*Paeonia officinalis* in crimson, rose, pink and white. Each clump was set in a round of cleared soil near the regularly-mown path and the soil around each was kept free from grass and weeds. Whether the paeonies would thrive without this attention I do not know although William Robinson suggested growing them in long grass cut down in August when the foliage was ripe.

Perhaps more in keeping are the columbines especially the blue *Aquilegia alpinum* and Miss Jekyll's 'Munstead White' (*A. vulgaris nivea*) which can occasionally be bought and then bred true from seed. Even the long-spurred hybrids do not look out of place and their airy blossoms will lend colour and charm for many weeks. So, too, will the perennial cornflower, the blue *Centaurea montana*, and neither this nor the columbines really need prepared beds. These and the other summer flowers should, however, be kept to the further reaches of the orchard where the grass need not be scythed until August. In the nearer parts the grass will be cut at the end of June when all the bulb foliage has died down.

We had bluebells to follow the wild tulip *sylvestris* in the grass—the ordinary wild bluebell of the beechwoods, and these can be bought from at least one specialist bulb firm. Where the larger, paler, garden varieties *Endymion* (*Scilla*) *hispanicus* are preferred they may be just as effectively used instead. They are, however, much more expensive to buy. Later blooms a North American bulb that looks in flower like a giant bluebell—*Camassia quamash* (*esculenta*), sending up pale starry spikes to a height of eighteen inches. The taller, lavender-starred *C. cusickii* and the deep blue *C. leichtlinii* are also good.

An old favourite that is little-grown today is the golden *Allium moly* of the onion family. Inoffensive of smell if not bruised, it carpets the grass in June with its bright golden umbels. I have seen *A. triquetrum* recommended as a wild garden plant and certainly it is very pretty with its drooping white bells. Its odour, however, is only slightly less pungent than that of the common wild garlic of British woodlands and some who have smelled it mingled with the heady but otherwise delightful scent of *Rhododendron griffithianum* and 'Loderi' in Cornish gardens have been nauseated. Plant instead the inoffensive white bluebell which it so much resembles.

Oriental poppies will grow in the orchard grass and look effective flaunting their orange and scarlet cups. The pink and white varieties are less often seen but are extremely pretty and should be mingled with the others to make a more softly coloured group. Most poppies do well in grass and it is worth scattering a packet or two of seed of the Shirley strain and the paeony-flowered 'Pink Beauty' where they will not be cut down by the June scything. Seed of the Flanders poppy may also be bought and its scarlet flowers are reminiscent of those of the wild poppy of our own cornfields.

Wild flowers such as Hedge Parsley and Meadowsweet may come uninvited into the wild orchard garden helping to capture the spirit of summer and making one reluctant to cut them down with the grass. Cut the grass must be, however, before it is flattened by the weather and the task made too difficult for scythe or rotoscythe. After the cutting is done the orchard may look a little bare for a time but that can be offset by the planting in the grass of two or three perpetual-flowering shrub roses such as 'Nevada' (cream), 'Marguerite Hilling' (rose-pink), 'Ballerina' (soft-pink) and 'Golden Wings' (yellow). Some of the taller trees, too, may be used as hosts for such informal climbing roses as 'The Garland' which has small upright bunches of sweetly-scented white rosette flowers, the pretty pink 'Debutante', and the larger flowered, creamy-white 'Felicité et Perpetue' that embowers so many cottages with its cool refreshing scent. 'Goldfinch', too, is good though its yellow soon fades to cream. For a true, bunch-flowered yellow I can think of none more charming than the May-flowering double yellow Banksian rose but it is not reliably hardy in the colder counties. These roses need little pruning. Indeed the Banksian must have none as it flowers on the shoots from last year's wood. They will probably need some support in the early years at any rate and this may conveniently be provided by a hoop or two of wire about the tree trunk into which the shoots may be tied.

Foxgloves are lovely in any wild gardens but in the orchard they must be grouped close to the tree boles or along the hedge-bank if they are to avoid being cut down with the grass before they have reached their best. Many good strains of foxglove are available but do please avoid the rightly named 'Monstrosa' with a bunch of flowers set in a deformed fashion on top of the stalk and also the 'Excelsior' strain with flowers all round the stem, completely voiding the natural foxglove grace.

Grouped similarly to the foxgloves, the Meadow Cranesbill—*Geranium pratense*—with its lovely blue flowers is a wild plant of great beauty. In the orchard garden it may be associated with the old-fashioned white Moon Daisy to make an unforgettable picture beneath the trees.

A pleasant point of interest for August comes from *Galtonia candicans*, the Summer Hyacinth, which carries its large creamy-white bells on stately stems quite four feet high. Another plant with an even longer season of beauty is the variegated Gladwyn Iris—*Iris foetidissima*—'Variegata' which has the usual beautiful seed-heads of the species (glistening orange berries in a handsome case the colour of pale bronze) with striking leaves of green and cream.

Colchicums planted around the trees are beautiful in September when they lift their white, lilac and pale purple cups above the grass to meet the downward sweep of the boughs that are heavy with the weight of reddening apples. They should be planted in July or August—the earlier the better—and will increase from year to year. Where they are grown the grass should be given a second cut about the third week in August so that it will not hide their chalices.

In an orchard there is not usually much room for additional trees or bushes. But where space can be found there are a few shrubs—in addition to the roses mentioned earlier—that can be included without spoiling the character of the place. One that I would not like to forego is the chaenomeles (cydonia) which in its blood-red or terra-cotta forms flowers earlier than the fruit-trees and adds a note of vivid colour that would otherwise be absent. Free-flowering forms that do not grow too large are the double 'Lady Moore', 'Rowallane Seedling' and the dwarf 'Simonii'. 'Knaphill Scarlet' and 'Boule de Feu' are also good. Essential pruning to prevent tangle consists of the spurring back of the long spiny shoots of new growth in late July.

The evergreen rhododendrons are not suitable for the orchard garden. Only the honeysuckle-flowered azaleas— the Ghent hybrids—have the necessary lightness of build and flower truss that is in keeping with the summery meadow-flower beauty of this particular kind of wild garden. There is also a lilac—the feathery-trussed Persian lilac, *Syringa persica*, in purple or white which fits in happily. So, too, do the mock-oranges. Their scented white blossom seems exactly what is needed among the greenery of leaves and grass in high summer.

Occasionally an old orchard tree may die and when the

stump has been grubbed up, or plugged with sodium chlorate and then fired, there arises the question, with what to replace it. A candidate that comes to mind is the silver-leafed weeping pear *Pyrus salicifolia pendula*. The fruit of this pear is hard and inedible but the charm of its white blossom, silver-grey leaves and gnarled branches are a delightful enough addition on their own account. Or one might add a flowering cherry. The more unsophisticated white-flowered varieties fit in better with pink and white apple blossom and the green-white foam of plum and damson than do the more artificial tones of 'Kanzan' and some of the pink varieties.

In all probability even an old and somewhat neglected orchard will yield more than enough fruit for the modern household. Even so the crop is a worthwhile one and though perhaps the wild gardener will not want to be troubled by the niceties of thinning and over-much pruning it is pleasant to have fruit of good quality and without unsightly blemishes. Grease-banding against pests is worth while.

Too much spraying quite apart from the trouble entailed can be definitely harmful as many fruit pests have predatory insects and mites which prey upon them. Only one spraying is really necessary in a semi-wild orchard such as we are discussing and this should be timed so as to disturb the natural control of pests by predators as little as possible. Spraying with *Captan* will help to protect against scab to which 'Cox's Orange Pippin', 'James Grieve' and 'Laxton's Superb' among other apples are susceptible. The 'William's' pear is also liable to this trouble. Aphis may be painted out with a paraffin and soft soap solution when the woolly manifestations appear.

Although the wild gardener who gardens in an orchard will not want to be burdened with over-much pruning it is as well to give the minimum attention necessary to keep the centres of the trees open, removing criss-crossing and

damaged wood. To prevent the trees becoming too tall
and the blossom being carried too high overhead with the
fruit consequently out of reach it is worth also shortening
the main branches to a third of their length and thereby
gaining a supply of scented apple logs for pleasant winter
burning. 'Worcester Pearmain', 'Blenheim Orange' and
'Lord Lambourne', however, should not have their
branches shortened in this way because they are tip-
bearers and removing the ends of the branches would
result in loss of fruit. Sawn off branches should be painted
with lead paint or *Arbrex 805* to prevent fungus invasion.

Pear trees may be dealt with in the same way as apples
but plums, fruiting cherries and damsons should not be
pruned until May. Such pruning should, however, be re-
stricted to the removal of dead or criss-cross shoots.

Even a starkly new bungalow can have its orchard
garden and I have seen the end of a long narrow back
garden of a suburban semi-detached house transformed
by four apple trees and a planting of white foxgloves and
bluebells. When planting fruit trees from scratch it is
important to remember that the root area of each must be
kept free from grass for the first five or six years. In the
wild garden this is a benefit as it enables primroses, violets, cowslips and colchicums to be well-established in the
root-circle of each tree before the grass is allowed to encroach.

For the planters of tiny orchards the family-tree idea
may have something to offer. Apple and pear trees are
available with separately grafted branches of compatible
varieties. Thus an eating apple tree might carry 'Laxton's
Epicure', 'Laxton's Fortune', 'Ellison's Orange', 'Worcester Pearmain', and 'Cox's Orange Pippin'.

Where there is more room a selection of bush trees on
dwarfing stocks will come into bearing early and still
leave room beneath their branches for the daffodils and
columbines of the wild garden. Good apples to choose for

succession would be 'Early Victoria', 'Lord Derby', 'Stirling Castle' and 'Lane's Prince Albert' to provide fruit for cooking purposes with 'Worcester Pearmain' and 'Cox's Orange Pippin' as eating apples. Pears might include 'William's', 'Conference' and 'Louise Bonne of Jersey' or 'Beurrée Hardy'. If there is room for only one plum tree 'Victoria', being self-pollinating, should be the choice, and I would always plant a damson such as 'Rivers's Early' for its beautiful frothy, greeny-white blossom as well as for its fruit which is so good for tarts or to make delectable damson cheese.

An extension of the orchard idea might be the planting of a small nuttery with either polyanthus primrose or coloured stemless primroses mingled with the purple drumstick *Primula denticulata*, grape hyacinths and Tenby daffodils (*Narcissus obvallaris*) as a purely spring garden. Polyanthus primulas need more attention in the way of bi-yearly division and feeding than do the *P. vulgaris* varieties so for a *wild* spring garden the latter are perhaps the better choice.

Good nuts to choose are 'Kentish Cob' ('Lambert's Filbert') and 'Pearson's Prolific'. Three bushes of each with the purple-leafed Filbert *Corylus maxima 'Atropurpurea'* and the non-cropping but autumn-and-winter-colourful witch-hazel *Hamamelis mollis* would make a useful and picturesque little nuttery.

CHAPTER FOUR

# Heathland Gardening

WHERE planning restrictions allow, new bungalows and houses are sometimes set amidst attractive heathland. Such development often occurs within three or four miles of town or city boundaries and is often an answer to the need of the more prosperous city-worker to 'get away from it all' and to return each evening to the fairly wide open spaces. Such properties, often with half an acre or more of heather, gorse, birch and scrub surrounding them, present something of a problem to the more garden-minded owners. It is both futile and expensive to try to tame these wildernesses—to try to make them conform to the suburban pattern of rose-garden, lawn and mixed border. Far more pleasing results are obtained by taking the best features of the existing heathland—the clumps of birch, the odd mountain-ash or thorn, the boulders and the heather and starting from there, adding only such plants as will be in keeping with the setting.

Paths, of course, there will have to be—preferably of shale or chippings—and these may follow the tracks worn by the sheep or foxes, the animal routes that skirted the gorse thickets and led to the birch covert; tracks that showed plainly amid the heather before the building began. There will have to be a drive, also, and this should at once strike a note in key with the character of the heathland garden. Like the paths it may be of shale, chippings or gravel and it may be banked on either side with heather. A short drive could be fringed by the lower-growing heaths such as the September-blooming double ling *Calluna* 'H. E. Beale' with its graceful spikes of lavender rosettes, the rosy-mauve *Erica* × *darleyensis* 'A. T. Johnson' and the white *E. mediterranea* 'W. T. Rackliff' for winter colour. This last is a particularly good heath with bright yet dark green foliage and will make dense, rounded bushes up to two feet in height. To flank a longer drive it may be planted in company with three-foot mounds of the bright rosy-purple *E. mediterranea* and the five-foot mossy-green *E. arborea alpina* which bears its ashen-white bells in April. *Erica lusitanica* flowers earlier and is distinctive with its fox-tail branches and smaller, sweetly scented bells that are just tinged with red. It is not hardy enough for the bleaker Midland and Northern areas where *E. arborea alpina* will be safer.

*Erica australis* is said to be tender. With us it has withstood nineteen degrees of frost (Fahrenheit) and cold off-the-sea winds. It has a white variety 'Mr. Robert'. I think they may be among those plants that prove tougher when grown in exposed, yet sunny and well-drained places than they do in lush, more sheltered spots. It is best to try one or two plants only of these varieties at first to see how they do in your garden before ordering more. The autumn-flowering *E. terminalis* (*stricta*) (3–4 feet) is normally hardy given full sun and good drainage yet it was killed in our garden in full shelter in the winter of 1962–63. Fully exposed bushes in much colder gardens survived. *E. terminalis* is a pleasing heath with dark, fuzzy outlines and pale pink flowers borne at the tips of the branches in August.

With these heaths may be associated the double gorse, *Ulex europaeus* '*Flore Pleno*' and the silvery-leafed *Elaeagnus* × *ebbingei*. When established this hybrid carries sweetly scented, silvery, tiny fuchsia-like flowers in November. It is a handsome and valuable shrub.

In the heathland garden, winter need never be dull. The alpine heath *Erica carnea* in its many varieties will spread great rugs of warmth and colour to glow through the gloom of the darkest winter day. The earliest to flower, in November is the pink 'Eileen Porter' and this will be followed by 'Winter Beauty', 'King George', 'Praecox' and 'Queen of Spain' in varying shades of rose. The widely-spreading, white 'Springwood' and its variety 'Springwood Pink' follow in mid-to-late January or early February according to district and season. With them flowers the compact 'Ruby Glow' which in bright carmine is one of the most vivid of the winter heaths and is a better 'doer' and to my mind an altogether more reliable plant than the rather similar 'Vivellii' though some people say 'Vivellii' flowers more freely. However, I have no complaints about 'Ruby Glow' in this respect. With the exception of the 'Springwood' varieties these heaths should be planted at nine inches apart. 'Springwood' and 'Springwood Pink' need a distance of eighteen inches from plant to plant. All need weeding for the first two years until they meet to form a close mat. Thereafter they should be sheared after flowering to keep their growth dense and so prevent invasion by fine grasses.

To give height and colour contrast, the witch-hazels cannot be bettered. They will flower well even in quite cold districts and in addition to the beautiful *Hamamelis mollis* and 'Jelena' the taller and slightly later-blooming *H. japonica arborea* might be grown. With the typical low-forking, almost V-shaped growth of the witch-hazels, *arborea* will grow to ten or fifteen feet. The ribbons of its flowers are more twisted than those of *mollis* and it has less scent. Starting to flower at the end of January when *mollis* is almost over, *arborea* carries on until the end of February or into March when it may suitably be accompanied by the rosy and white varieties of *Daphne mezereum*. This daphne does very well in moist peaty ground but in the drier more sandy heathlands it needs a large flat stone placed over its root area to retain the moisture.

Not often seen but very much in character in such gardens are the sarcococcas. Rather inconspicuous in their creamy flower tufts they are far from inconspicuous in the haunting sweetness of their scent which is distilled in the air by the thin January sunshine. *Sarcococca ruscifolia* and *S. humilis* make dark green bushes about three feet in height and will grow and slowly spread in the roughest places. *S. hookeriana digyna* is a taller, more graceful shrub which is worth a place near the house.

Some of the early rhododendrons are at home in the heath garden. Where there are birches or other deciduous trees they should be sited among them for shelter. Sandy heathy soils need little preparation for them to succeed, although where the soil is very light added humus should be incorporated in the form of coarse peat. Too acid a soil —such as the black peat of some moorland areas—needs the addition of sand and neutralized horticultural peat.

Such rhododendrons as the December-January blooming 'Nobleanum', the February flowering willow-leafed *lutescens* which is so lovely in its deep primrose F.C.C. form, the rosy-mauve 'Praecox' and 'Emasculum' and the rosy 'Tessa' are very much in keeping with the character of the garden. They may be followed by the small-leafed *racemosum* with its upright racemes of pale pink flowers. Farrer's famous dwarf form of this species is, however, too small to compete with the heather without more supervision and cultivation than is warranted in a rather rough, wild, heath or moorland garden such as we are visualizing. The larger forms will best suit our purpose and should be group-planted, three or four together at a distance of a couple of feet apart, for effect. Moreover, such grouping will enable the individual members to benefit from the mutual shelter and help them better to withstand the weather. With *Rhododendron racemosum*, the neat dark-leafed 'Blue Diamond' and the lavender-blue 'Augfast' will look well. They, too, should have the benefit of group planting. Where one can spare the time or has the labour available to prepare a drift-shaped bed (eradicating all heather and grass and thoroughly cleansing the ground of roots) it is rewarding to plant a mass of the low-growing dwarf rhododendrons from the moorlands of China. Such species as *intricatum* and *impeditum* in lavender, the white *microleucum*, the yellow *chryseum* and rose-purple *lysolepis* group well and, huddled together for protection as in their native home, will withstand the worst that the winters can do. An unexpected delight is occasioned in early autumn when many of these dwarfs put on a second showing to heighten the beauty of the indigenous ling (*Calluna vulgaris*).

Many heathland gardens are sited in exposed and sometimes bleak places and do not offer the ornamental cherries a hospitable home. Nor are the garden cherries really in keeping. Much more in character are the amelanchiers (Snowy Mespilus) which are lighter in habit and bear their airy white blossoms among the downy beauty of their unfolding coppery leaves. *Amelanchier laevis* is even better than *A. canadensis* and I would also grow both *A. asiatica* and *oblongifolia* which are still more striking in habit and flower. All species colour well in autumn.

Apart from the birches—which, if there are none already on the site, should certainly be introduced—the sorbus (Mountain Ash) family are extremely good heathland garden trees. The native rowan, *Sorbus aucuparia*, is delightful in August when its branches are weighted with glowing orange berries to echo the tones of its already colouring leaves. Birds, however, soon strip the berries. Luckily our feathered friends are not so eager to try the less familiar pink and yellow fruited forms. *S.a.* 'Old

Pink' and *S.a.* Xanthocarpa (orange-yellow) are reliable followed by such later forms as the stiff habited *Sorbus decora* which bears its large sealing-wax berries towards November when, oddly, the birds do not seem to take them. Perhaps they have turned their attention to hawthorn and holly. A good match for *S. decora* is *cashmeriana* with glistening white berries almost as big as old-fashioned glass marbles. A Chinese species *S. hupehensis* is also lovely, with ferny, greyish foliage that colours to orange and large hanging clusters of small white berries that turn to pink and last well into the winter.

The weeping form of the silver birch should be planted where there is room, in addition to the existing birches. With its distinctive form it should stand alone, away from the other trees. It is worth clearing the heather or bracken around it and planting a few clumps of daffodils. Later the grass may be allowed to creep back to its base. For its extra-tall, creamy trunk and golden rain of October leaf-fall I would plant also *Betula ermanii*. Where there is a patch of damp peat or boggy ground opportunity arises to plant the North American river birch, *B. nigra* with its shaggy dark bark and soft green foliage. The Swedish *B. pendula dalecarlica* has an extra-white trunk and 'Young's Weeping Birch' *B.p.* 'Youngii' might also be used to give contrast of habit.

If the ground is not too acid, seed may be scattered or bulbs imported and bluebells may be persuaded to grow beneath the birches to echo the hyacinth tones of the dwarf blue rhododendrons mentioned earlier. To intensify this wood-smoke haze a few of the blue-toned hardy hybrids might be added as background. 'Blue Danube', 'Susan' and 'Blue Peter' are all suitable and may be succeeded by the fine old 'Fastuosum Flore Pleno'.

By June the potentillas should be in flower. With some of the species roses and heathers, these form the mainstay of the heathland garden throughout the summer. Almost

3    Giant endymion and a good strain of *Aquilegia alpina* naturalized in the woodland in the late A. T. Johnson's garden at Bulkeley Mill.

4  *Ligularia clivorum* 'Desdemona', a striking moist-ground plant in my own garden.

all are good. Among the best are the soft yellow 'Moon-light' (Manelys) which makes a mound of pale green and yields its buttercup-shaped flowers from May to November; the bright yellow 'Katherine Dykes' and *Potentilla fruticosa vilmoriniana* with silver leaves and creamy flowers. To hump itself over a flat rock or boulder, the low-growing *P.f. mandshurica* is most attractive with purple-stemmed white flowers and silver-grey leaves. Striking, too, is the newer 'Tangerine' the yellow petals of which are tipped with flame to give a bright and glowing effect.

From mid-May onwards the species roses give colour and some scent. Most suitable are the yellow × *cantabrigiensis* and deeper 'Canary Bird'. Even the semi-double *spinosissima* hybrid 'Frühlingsgold' is free and abandoned enough to grace the wild. One or two of the sweet-briars should be grown for their scented foliage after rain. I like especially the coppery 'Lady Penzance' and crimson 'Meg Merrilees'. Both bear a good crop of hips later in the year. The foliage of the wild white and pale yellow Burnet roses also has a refreshing fragrance. A good cultivated form is *Rosa spinosissima* 'Altaica'. Also pleasing to the nose is *R. primula* with small yellow flowers reminiscent of the potentilla and a pervading scent of incense. Blooming only a little later and, unlike the roses so far mentioned, flowering on and on throughout the summer, the Japanese Rugosa roses are vigorous growers that do well in wild conditions. To these virtues they add an autumn leaf-tint like sunlit ripened corn and large, tomato-shaped fruit. Best for the purpose are 'Alba' with orange-red hips that contrast pleasantly with the later crop of single white flowers. 'Frau Dagmar Hastrup' with soft-pink flowers lit by creamy stamens, and the crimson-purple 'Rubra'. The double-flowered forms would be out of keeping with the simplicity of so open and wild a setting.

For height one might grow also *R. moyesii* of the blood-
D

red flowers and flagon-shaped fruits and the brighter 'Geranium'. One must take care, though, not to overplant. Simplicity is the keynote. The background of the garden is to be found in the great stretches of heather, the birches and the belts of soft-toned rhododendrons. The roses are the highlights, spot-lighting the summer season. So a bush or two here and there with perhaps a drift of a good single variety such as *rugosa* 'Alba' or 'Rubra' is just what is needed. Indiscriminate or unrelated planting could give only a spotty effect. Unity of theme is important in a garden. To introduce too many unrelated subjects would ruin a wild garden.

Autumn is perhaps the finest season in the heathland garden. As the moor-purple drifts of ling spread to the skyline, the scarlet and gold of berry and leaf take over the theme. Low drifts of the marble-berried pernettyas with their pink, white and crimson fruits may be heightened by the introduction of the rose-madder leaves and lilac fruits of *Callicarpa giraldiana*. To ensure freedom of berry in the pernettyas, the male form of *Pernettya mucronata* should be included in any group. Two or three specimens of callicarpa, planted together, will fruit more freely than a single plant.

*Cotoneaster* 'Cornubia' is a splendid berrying plant with a graceful habit, neat dark leaves and large sprays of vivid scarlet fruits. Quite different but equally attractive is *C. conspicuus* which the plant-hunter the late Frank Kingdon-Ward described as a 'bubbling cauldron of berries'. Tiny in leaf and of arching growth, this species mounds itself into a shrub of three or four feet and from October on is covered with bright red berries. To give variety and to foil the birds which, as always, seem distrustful of an unusual colour form, the yellow-fruited *C.* × *exburiensis* or *frigidus* 'Fructu Luteo' might be grown. These rather similar forms are both graceful in growth with slim, willow-like evergreen leaves. A late-flowering species *C.*

*serotinus* which carries its typical white hawthorn-like flowers in August is correspondingly late in ripening its warm red berries which consequently last through the winter.

Berries in autumn are delightful but berries that last through the winter are the most valuable of all. Their scarlet and crimson, buttercup and orange, sparkles in the frost and glows through the winter damp with a cheeriness that warms in even the worst weather.

The holly-like berries of the skimmia last not only through the winter itself but are often carried on from season to season so that their colour becomes noticeable in September when the summer flowers fade and remains to make a bright background when the daffodils are in bloom. After that no one notices the berries because the yearly pageant of large-scale colour has begun. They are there, however, just the same—ready to pick at Christmas-time when holly berries are few and the price of holly in the shops is high.

Some species of skimmia are unisexual so both male and female bushes must be grown unless a near neighbour has a convenient male. For small gardens the best solution may be to grow *Skimmia* × *foremanni* which is hermaphro-ditic and may be relied upon to berry freely on its own. Other hermaphrodites which one may perhaps come across in a local nursery are 'Veitchii' and 'Wisley Red'. Skimmias are pleasant in their scented flowers as well as in their berries. For anyone who would like to grow the finest red-budded flowering form—a male, alas—*S. japonica rubella* is the one to choose.

Perhaps no berried shrub has occasioned more dis-appointment than the brilliant *P. coccinea lalandii* the fine orange berries of which are borne early and readily gobbled by the eager birds. Those species of which the berries ripen later are more likely to remain untouched. One of the showiest of these is the *P. atalantioides* with darker orange-scarlet fruits. The berries of this species are smaller than those of *lalandii* and so freely carried as to make one think of the little round sweetmeats known as 'hundreds and thousands'. They do not ripen until mid-November and generally remain in beauty until January or longer. Grown in the open it makes a high, mounded bush with fine dark evergreen leaves. Its white, hawthorn-like flowers in June and July are also attractive.

The golden-berried 'Knaphill Buttercup' makes a pleasing contrast. Yellow-berried shrubs are not often planted and this variety is generous enough with its fruit to cause a shock of delighted surprise when one sees them gleaming handsomely against the dark foliage.

For foreground planting, at the edge of a path, a dwarf evergreen offers brilliant fruit. It is *Viburnum davidii* with large, leathery, ribbed leaves and bright turquoise berries which are unisexual so that both male and female forms must be planted. Glorious in the winter sunlight are the ripening fruits of the strawberry tree, *Arbutus unedo*. Shading from green through sour apricot to orpiment-orange and finally dull crimson these combine most attractively with the parchment-coloured hanging bunches of lily-of-the-valley like flowers. It does not mind lime in the soil. Hollies are distinctive both for value of their dark evergreen shapes and for the beauty of their berries. Some are unisexual and so both male and female must be planted to ensure berrying. The form known as 'J. C. Van Tol' however is self-berrying and therefore a good one to choose. The variegated hollies, though attractive in a more formal setting, would be completely out of place in the wild garden. Conifers, too, are important though care must be taken not to plant too many and so ruin the character of the heathland. Perhaps the Scots Pine—*Pinus sylvestris*—is the most suitable, the rugged scaly stems of mature specimens making a perfect background to heather and dwarf rhododendron. Quicker to reach maturity, the larch is also in keeping and in an open setting takes on a picturesquely windswept shape. Beautiful in spring when the fresh green tufts of new foliage break from the pliant branches, it is lovely, too, in autumn when that same foliage turns soft apricot before falling to lay a russet carpet over path and turf.

With the exception of the rhododendrons and most of the heaths (except lime-tolerant *Erica carnea mediterranea* and its hybrids and *terminalis*) which do not thrive in chalky areas, the plants that we have mentioned as being suitable for a heathland garden will be equally at home in the wild garden on the downs. There, autumn colour of berry and leaf will be just as important and the shrub roses of summer equally happy. I would add, though, all viburnum species from the wild guelder rose with its rather poor flower-heads and scarlet jujubes of fruit in autumn to the more sophisticated *Viburnum plicatum* var. *tomentosum* 'Mariesii' with its striking tabular growth and lovely white lacecap flowers. The upright habit of the winter-flowering *V.* × *bodnantense* will contrast well with a free-growing bush of the winter jasmine—*Jasmine nudiflorum*—its whippy, yellow-starred branches allowed to cascade naturally over a convenient boulder.

On the chalk the wild green hellebore—*Helleborus foetidus*—with its dark, deep-fingered leaves can take the place of some of the heathers, although the winter heaths and the taller *Erica mediterranea* may still be relied upon to succeed. Cowslips will do well in the short turf and earlier the lilac February-flowering crocus with its bright orange stigmata, *Crocus tomasinianus*, will seed itself far and wide—a planting of a hundred corms over the years increasing to several thousand. This crocus takes three years to flower from seed and thereafter increases by compound interest. It is one of the finest floral investments the wild gardener can make.

Brooms will be quite at home in the downland garden,

as indeed they would be in the heathland. The early-blooming *Cytisus praecox* and its white variety have now been joined by various coloured hybrids of which the pink and red 'Hollandia' is one of the best. Later 'Moonlight', 'Golden Queen', 'Burkwoodii', 'Johnson's Crimson', 'Enchantress' and the rest offer a wide choice of colour forms. This theme of spring may be taken up again in late summer by *Spartium junceum* the narcissus-scented, rush-stemmed Spanish Broom with its upright spikes of golden pea-blossom.

Of the berried shrubs, the spindle-berries are particularly at home on chalk. The native *Euonymus europaeus* with its rose-coloured capsules and orange seeds should certainly be grown and might be accompanied by its purple-leafed form, *E.e. atropurpureus* and *E.e.* 'Red Cascade' of arching habit. For fine rose to scarlet autumn leaf-colour, *E. alatus* should also be grown, while I would not like to be without the tall *yedoensis* which has perhaps the brightest seed capsules of all in 'shocking pink'. It is difficult to have too many spindle trees. Their slender growth occupies but little space and they fruit more freely for being in company.

In place of the pine and larch recommended for the heathland garden one might plant the juniper whose natural home is on the chalk. Dwarf varieties such as the prostrate *Juniperus sabina tamariscifolia* and the widely spreading *J.* × *media pfitzeriana* in its glaucous and golden forms would contrast well with the taller *J. communis*. The only junipers which do not do well on chalk are *J. recurva* and its sub-species *J.r. coxii* with its soft red shaggy trunk and semi-weeping foliage. These most beautiful trees will do well in the wild wood-garden but should not be planted in too exposed or bleak a situation.

More common shrubs such as the rose-red Flowering Currant, *Ribes* 'Atrosanguineum', the Golden Currant, *R. aureum*, with its subtler charm and the fuchsia-flowered

*R. speciosum* are not to be despised. Many such homely beauties are well-known just because they are good doers and it is the burgeoning bounty of thriving, healthy shrubs that with a few good trees and such herbaceous and bulbous plants as will naturalize *en masse* that add so considerably to the charm of the wild garden.

Another currant-like shrub which is lifted right out of the rut by its fragrance is *Osmaronia (Nuttallia) cerasiformis* with ribes-like racemes of deliciously scented white flowers against fresh green foliage in early spring. Forsythias, too, are good—especially in informal surroundings and to the better-known bright gold *Forsythia × intermedia* 'Spectabilis' and the paler, tangled *F. suspensa* may be added *F.* 'Lynwood' with extra-large deep yellow flowers.

# CHAPTER FIVE

# Streamside and Pool

THERE is nothing, one may think, more charming than to have a stream of running water in the garden; to hear it gurgle and chuckle over the pebbles; to see the trees and sky reflected on its surface; to gaze into the depths of its clear, dark pools. Surely, one assumes, there can be no more perfect setting for a wild garden.

The assumption, of course, is right. Running water in the garden is delightful. In a good wild garden it is enchantment. But, as always, between the dream and its realization there may be considerable hard work.

Not all streams have sparkling clarity. Some are choked with waterweed—fouled and dammed with sticks and the accumulated rubbish of years. One may be lucky and have a clear, pebble-bedded brook, a peat-brown mountain stream, or a slower, winding sandy-bottomed rivulet. On the other hand one may have the merest ditch or drainage culvert that needs digging out and widening before one can begin to make wild garden plantings on its banks. No matter! So long as there is water, the potential is there.

Most streams have a problem. Either the flow is too slow and waterweeds, rushes, wild iris and even one's own more prolific plantings choke the watercourse or it is too swift and one's treasures are perpetually swept away. The bed of a sluggish stream needs cleaning at least once a year. Overthick plantings must be thinned, obstructions removed and the stream-bed raked to remove dead leaves, weed and the odd tin can or other nuisance. Above all one must be careful what one plants by such waters. The glorious lysichitums with their golden or ivory arum-spathes and tropical banana leaves have rootstocks in proportion. It takes a strong man to hack through and uproot a single plant of lysichitum so they must be confined either to a back-water or to a pool too wide for them to bridge.

Most streams, at some time or other, are liable to flood but the swift-running mountain watercourse is the worst of all. The banks of one such between Beddgelert and Caernarvon in North Wales are lined for several miles with a fine montbretia, the result of one gardener's attempt (successful at last, I am glad to say) to establish a planting in his own waterside paradise just below the Nant Mill Falls.

Even at Bulkeley Mill in the Conway Valley the usually sluggish mill leat in times of flood carried away primulas, irises and other streamside plants. The answer to this problem lies in the careful choice and preparation of planting sites. It is useless to ram plants into the bank. They should be set, if possible, in natural dips and hollows of moist or boggy ground running back from the water. Failing this one should excavate irregular planting basins and hollows using the soil, reinforced with large stones to make dams to hold back the flood water. The level of the planting stations can be suited to the needs of the plants to be set therein. Most primulas, for instance, enjoy moist soil but do not like to have their roots in water so their beds will be higher than those intended for *Iris laevigata* or *I. pseudacorus*, the native yellow flag, which like to have their roots actually in the water.

As with other forms of wild gardening it is also necessary to prepare planting sites in order to give the plants a good start. One cannot just ram plants among coarse grasses and weeds and expect them to grow. Under such conditions the weeds and grasses always win.

One of the dangers of wild gardening is over-planting and of nowhere is this more true than at the waterside. The setting is so tempting. One thinks one simply must have this or another clump of that and before one realizes it the original character of the place has gone. Sometimes this may not matter. A drainage culvert in an indifferent setting widened and planted to an almost tropical luxuriance could only be improved. Rodgersias, primulas, irises, astilbes—even a giant rheum—certainly the lace-cap hydrangeas and waterside ferns will create atmosphere where there was none before. On the other hand a pretty little stream on the outskirts of a wood or tumbling through a boulder-strewn valley needs very little enhancement. Perhaps the addition of a willow—not necessarily of a weeping variety—or the tupelo, *Nyssa sylvatica*—which is so lovely in its autumn colouring when established—a few Kingcups, with a patch of the purple drumstick primula set back a little way from the water's edge, the deeper purple form of the Ladysmock—*Cardamine macrophylla*—with a belt of the yellow water iris, a smaller group of the deep purple *Iris chrysographes* and a subtle planting of the tall *Primula florindae* with its giant, powdery-yellow, scented cowslip bells. One has to be so careful, to add a planting here and there, feeling one's way as it were and all the time remaining aware of the threat so inherent in wild gardening—that of spoiling an already perfect scene by over-embellishment.

Native primroses are a joy by the water-side and always to be encouraged. Often they will seed and so plant themselves in just the right position, wedged between two boulders above a tiny waterfall or bedded in the turf at the water's edge, their pale starry faces mirrored in the slowly-moving water.

Weeds at the waterside can often be a problem; the moist ground encourages their spread and they are apt to swamp the less robust plants that one might introduce. There are some families of moisture-loving plants, however, that grow more thickly and strongly even than the weeds. These are the ones to plant on difficult ground. For this purpose the lysichitums mentioned earlier are excellent, especially if one can plant them on the margin of a stretch of water so wide (nine to ten feet or so) that they are unlikely to clog it. A wise precaution would be to bound the stretch of bank allotted to them by a sheet of iron or plastic sunk to a three-foot depth. The yellow-flowered species, *Lysichitum americanum*, will be known to most people by its glistening golden spathes. These are followed by two- to three-foot ribbed leaves of soft green. After flowering the green spadix flops to the ground and decays to a jelly-like slime in which the seeds ripen. Plenty of young lysichitums will presently appear, to be separated and re-planted if one wants to increase one's stock. On the other hand control of their spread is achieved by removing the young plants at this stage. Not everyone likes the somewhat shrill gold of *L. americanum* though most people find the leaves handsome and valuable to supply a dramatic note of form and texture by the summer waterside. The white satiny spathes of *L. camtschatcense*, however, displease no one. They are like a giant arum lily and just as handsome. Their leaves are similar to those of *L. americanum* but perhaps a little smaller and of a striking glaucous blue. For foliage value alone the lysichitums are among the most valuable of wet ground plants.

Of smaller proportions but equally good as weed-smother are the astilbes which in moist ground mat to form a close raft of roots and stems through which no undesirables can penetrate. With their divided leaves and feathery plumes of flowers, the astilbes are a pleasing sight —especially if they are planted in drifts of graded colour.

Good varieties to choose are the lilac purple 'Cattleya', deep rose 'Granat', bright pink 'Rhineland' and white 'Irrlicht'. Two later-blooming varieties, the lilac 'Amethyst' and pink 'Tamarix' are useful to prolong the season. Where a shorter growing astilbe is needed *A. chinensis* growing only to eighteen inches with fluffy lilac spires of flowers is strong growing and appealing.

The yellow *Lysimachia punctata* is a fine colonizer to keep down weeds and is very pleasing with its spikes of treacle-gold flowers above the soft green foliage. Quite different in character but a splendid weed suppressor for damp ground at the side of a pond or stream, the ligularias have striking dark-green rounded leaves, large and lined with purple. The classic daisy sprays of *Ligularia clivorum* 'Desdemona' and 'Othello' are bright orange. Nearby the three-foot spires of the purple loosestrife, *Lythrum salicaria*, would be effective. This is another good weed suppressor and will grow either on the drier parts of the bank, in boggy ground or actually in shallow water. The rosy-red 'Beacon', deep pink 'Brightness' and purple *L. virgatum* 'Dropmore Purple' are representative named varieties.

Irises, too, are close in growth and where they are planted near together weeds are discouraged. Not all irises are water loving but among the best and easiest are the native yellow *Iris pseudacorus* and its paler form *bastardii* both of which will grow with their roots in water at the edge of the stream or pond. Even more attractive are the Siberian irises, *I. sibirica*, which will do well in damp ground at the margin although they should not be grown actually in the water. Very pleasing is the graceful old variety 'Perry's Blue' with slim-petalled flowers of soft blue velvet. Some of the newer hybrids have larger flowers but none are more graceful. Among the best are the blues 'Cool Spring' and 'Mountain Lake' and the purples 'Caesar's Brother' and 'Tropic Night'. 'Helen

Astor' is a very good pinky red. There are two easily obtainable whites 'Snow Queen' and 'Wisley White'. With them can be associated the yellow *I. forrestii*, a more slender and graceful plant than *I. pseudacorus* but smaller in stature than the Siberian irises. It is near in habit to the nearly black *I. chrysographes*—a favourite of mine. This species spreads well and a good patch of its velvety dark flowers with the gold veining on their falls is a sight worth remembering. There is an unmarked variety *rubella*, a dark claret, which I have grown also. It, too, is a good 'doer' but it is not really as eye-catching as the type.

*Iris laevigata* is well-known as a water-plant for ponds. It likes to grow in shallow water at the edge of a pond and will grow equally well in a rather still back-water of a stream. Six inches is about the maximum depth at which it should be planted and where no suitably shallow planting pocket exists one may easily be made by building an underwater shelf with boulders, fronting it with larger boulders and ramming in upside-down turves to form a good layer of soil in which to plant the iris. The turves will probably need to be weighted with stones. Equally lovely with their great clematis-like heads are the single-flowered varieties of *I. kaempferi*. Perhaps the self-purples and the whites show up best in a wild-setting but almost all are attractive.

Plants with distinctive leaves are particularly valuable for waterside effect. We have discussed several already—the lysichitums, irises and ligularias—and where a single massive specimen is wanted one of the giant rhubarbs such as *Rheum palmatum* 'Atropurpureum', the large rhubarb leaves of which are lined with crimson, will be striking in effect. The gunneras with their six-foot leaves are too big for any but the wild garden on the grandest possible scale though there are places by the waterside in large estates or public parks where they will not dwarf their surroundings and where their use is fitting and right.

By a sheltered pond or stream where there is some shade and protection from strong wind the rodgersias should do well. When they are not happy they do not flower freely so it is worth finding the right conditions to suit them. Not rampant at first, the rodgersias take two or three years to become established. Their creeping underground shoots eventually form a strong mat that will effectively banish weeds. The initial planting should be at two to three feet apart. *Rodgersia aesculifolia* has leaves rather like those of a horse chestnut, deeply fingered and about a foot and a half across. In July it sends up spiraea-like plumes, three feet or more in height and blush-white in colour. *R. pinnata* 'Superba' has similarly fingered leaves on stems up to three feet high and, even more handsome, purple-bronze in colour to complement the deep-rose flower plumes. The two species are effective if planted so that a drift of one merges into the other. They are plants for moist ground and should not be planted with their roots actually in water.

Less common and enjoying similar conditions, the podophyllums should be more often seen. With leaves rather like those of the rodgersia species mentioned, *Podophyllum emodii majus* has shell-pink, anemone-flowers followed by large oval, scarlet seed pods. It is not a vigorous colonizer but will spread slowly, in time forming a satisfying patch.

Invaluable as ground cover and also for the colourful beauty of their whorled and tiered heads of flowers, the Asiatic primulas are among the loveliest of all subjects for waterside planting. Moreover they always look exactly right, whatever the setting. Perhaps it is their affinity with our native primrose and cowslip; perhaps it is their essential grace and easy blend of colour values, but they never seem garish and always give a sense of the wild rather than of the over-cultivated garden confines. Easily raised in quantity from seed sown in winter and allowed to weather alternate frost and thaw, a selection of species is most rewarding. These may be either grown in patches of one kind or drifts of different colour merging into one another.

Of these easy primulas, *rosea* is the first to flower in spring. It is dwarfer than the others and very pretty with heads of bright rose pink on six-inch stems. It will be followed by the golden *helodoxa*, apricot *bulleyana* and *pulverulenta* with elegant tiers of magenta flowers on powdered mealy stems. In spite of its colour, *pulverulenta* is a primula of quality with none of the coarseness of *japonica*'s hearty leaves, fat stems and flowers. *Primula iaponica*, though, is good on its own, when it should be grown in drifts of its various colour forms, magenta, brick, pink and white. Apart from the type *pulverulenta* has some glorious varieties in shades of pink from deep rose to palest blush—all with an attractive golden eye. These are the forms arising from seed of the Bartley strain, packets of which may be bought. The yellow cowslip-like *sikkimensis* and the later *florindae*, mentioned earlier, are also attractive at the waterside.

I do not like to see the double-flowered kingcup in the wild garden—in fact I do not care for it at all because it seems so completely lacking in the usual purity and clarity of outline which one finds in the single form. There is, however, a larger form of the native *Caltha palustris* known as 'Tyerman's Variety' with larger golden cups and a touch of bronze in the leaf. This should be planted in addition to the wildling, a gleaming patch of which in the May sunshine is hard to beat. There is also an attractive white variety, *alba*, but this is not as vigorous as the type and should be planted in a group about nine inches apart. The Water Musk—*Mimulus luteus*—is as characteristic of the summer waterside as the kingcup is of spring. This native will usually increase from year to year without help but the superior 'A. T. Johnson's Variety' which bears flowers of velvety wallflower red just margined with gold, needs to be dug up each spring and replanted in the same site. Without this attention its simply disappears. So, too, does the coppery 'Burnettii' and the rose-pink, yellow-throated × *bartonianus*. The red *cardinalis*, however, is usually as easy as *luteus* and even seeds itself giving yellow seedlings as well as scarlet.

The two inhabitants of northern water-meadows and streamside banks are so delightful and characterful that they should be planted by every stretch of wild waterside. They are the pale yellow globe-flower, *Trollius europaeus*, and the Water Avens, *Geum rivale*, of which 'Leonard's Variety' is a cultivated form, with nodding bonnets that are larger and a brighter rosy-salmon than the type.

So far we have thought mainly of herbaceous plants. There is at least one bulb—*Leucojum aestivum*—the Loddon Lily—a rare native of British streamside banks, which does well by water. In late April and May it bears on eighteen-inch stems three swinging bells of white tipped with green just like the little lampshade-shaped flowers of the dwarfer *L. vernum* which flowers with the snowdrops in January.

In damp meadowland near the stream or pool the fritillary may be planted and with luck it may naturalize itself. With stems no thicker than those of a harebell and hanging dice-box bells either chequered in mauve and purple or else plain white it is a fairy plant and it is worth any amount of perseverance to get it to establish itself.

Moist soil near the water but above its highest level suits several North American species of erythronium—the Dog's Tooth Violet—with their turncap, miniature-lily flowers. Various white forms of these are available, the elegant creamy *Erythronium californicum* and the large hybrid 'White Beauty' both with central zones of colour at the throat. Unfortunately, the equally lovely pink *revolutum* and its hybrid 'Pink Beauty' simply cannot be

5　The yellow spathes of the bog arum *Lysichitum americanum* make a glowing picture in early spring at Bulkeley Mill.

6   The creamy-pink plumes and bronze leaves of *Rodgersia aesculifolia*
are decorative in summer in marshy ground.

obtained in this country at present. This is a great pity because all increase easily and can be raised from seed although they take five years to flower from sowing. The sight of drifts of the pink, echoing the white, dancing in the breeze beneath the branches of a thin waterside copse and reflected in the water is so enchanting that one hopes every effort will be made to reintroduce the pink forms to this country and to make them more generally available.

A good shrub for the waterside is the exochorda, the Pearl Bush, with graceful spraying branches from which the tight pearl-like white buds open into attractive snowy flowers. *Exochorda racemosa* is the one most generally in commerce.

Many people enjoy bamboos for their tropical air of jungle luxuriance. They must be chosen with care, however, or the jungle may get out of hand. Several safe species do exist, though, and they are no less beautiful than their rampant fellows. *Sinarundinaria murielae* is extremely graceful with ten-foot stems, arched at the top, and lovely, fresh green foliage. *S. nitida* is similar but with indigo stems which show up better than do the green ones of *murielae*. Both are hardy. For really large leaves choose *Pseudosasa japonica* (*Bambusa metake*) which may reach twelve to fifteen feet in a sheltered place.

The willows, of course, are the trees that most people associate with the waterside. *Salix chrysocoma* is the best known of the weeping forms. In fact if one refers to a 'weeping willow' it is taken for granted that this is the species meant. Lovely it is, too, with its yellow stems of trailing leaves that in spring unfold so fresh a green and later take on a bluish tinge. It does in time make a big specimen and so is only suitable for quite large stretches of wild garden or water. The Asiatic *S. matsudana* 'Pendula' is smaller-growing and though lacking the bright golden shoots of *chrysocoma* is nonetheless a most attractive

E

waterside subject. Another good small willow of weeping habit is the American *S. purpurea* 'Pendula' with purple bark and graceful glaucous leaves.

Pussy catkins, silver furred at first and later yellowing to resemble fluffy Easter chicks, are the main charm of the native *S. caprea*, the Palm or Goat Willow. If one keeps one's eyes open as one goes about the countryside in January one will often find forms already in catkin. A cutting from one of these taken with a heel will strike readily in damp soil and eventually enable one to have its desirably early catkins for one's own. Larger catkins, equally early and with a pinky flush are borne on the purple-stemmed *S. daphnoides* which in time makes a small tree. Pollarded annually to a foot-high stump it will not be able to yield its catkins but its violet stems with their bluish plum-bloom will make an effective contrast to the yolk-yellow shoots of *S. vitellina* so treated. Such cut-back shrubs are colourful in the wintry sunlight. Another subject for the same treatment is the crimson dogwood, *Cornus alba sibirica* with winter shoots of brilliant crimson. There is also a yellow-barked species *C. stolonifera flaviramea*. A little plantation of pollarded willows and dogwoods in moist or boggy ground may be underplanted with moisture-loving primulas such as *helodoxa* (the golden marsh primula), *sikkimensis* and *florindae* to give a long season of colour and interest.

For an unusual note of emphasis *Metasequoia glyptostroboides*, the dawn-age redwood, is a deciduous conifer of great beauty that does well in moist but not swampy places. Its feathery foliage, soft green in summer, in autumn turns to apricot, gold and orange. For really boggy ground the Swamp Cypress, *Taxodium distichum*, is a wiser choice. Not unlike the metasequoia, its autumn tint is richly rufous.

Water lilies are often among the *desiderata* of the gardener who has a stretch of water in his territory. Only the wild Brandy Bottles (the yellow nuphars) will grow in a running stream but where a fairly still pool can be made by widening and damming the watercourse various of the nymphae can be persuaded to grow, their roots packed between two thick turves and scurely bound with string before being lowered to the muddy pool bottom.

For deep water of two to three feet one may choose the large pomegranate red 'Attraction', the pale rose *Nymphae marliacea carnea*, the primrose *N.m. chromatella*, 'Rose Nymph' and the white *N. tuberosa* 'Poestlingberg'. Shallower conditions suit the rosy-orange 'Aurora', the deep red 'Escarboucle' and 'Froebeli', the copper-yellow 'Graziella', the rose-crimson 'James Brydon', the lovely deep pink 'Rose Arey' and the pinky-copper 'Sioux'.

# CHAPTER SIX

# Quarries, Ruins and Cliffs

In these days when building land is short one cannot neglect the disused quarry site. Such sites usually afford shelter from the wind on two or three sides and the exposed strata of rock, particularly if weathered and partly clothed with ivy, gorse or heather, make an attractive background for a house or bungalow. It is a difficult site to garden conventionally but it is full of possibilities for wild gardening.

An initial difficulty lies in the shallow depth of soil overlying the rock. In fact much of the site may be down to the bare rock where the actual quarrying has been done. To import soil to cover the whole area would be expensive but by importing enough to give a cover of about a foot to one's main planting sites one can effect a considerable saving and at the same time get results. If the basic rock is either limestone, chalk or sandstone it is a comparatively easy matter to excavate planting holes with a pick-axe and to break the rock into small rubble. With soil incorporated, this makes an excellent rooting medium for most plants. Granite, however, is so hard that excavation may be almost impossible and here one must limit much of one's planting to shallow-rooters such as heaths and geranium species and plant trees and shrubs only where suitable fissures or natural depressions already exist ready to be filled with good soil. Even here, provided suitable subjects are chosen, the plants will readily seed about; the seeds some-how finding suitable crevices or soil pockets and the seed-lings thrusting their roots into any available cracks, ex-tracting nourishment from the bare rocks and generally managing to grow into fine specimens. Mountain ash, buddleia, cotoneaster species and brooms are particularly good at naturalizing in this way, establishing themselves and colonizing in what might at first seem to be the most unpromising conditions. Other shrubs which will seed themselves and so increase are the single-flowered varieties of rugosa rose such as 'Frau Dagmar Hastrüp', 'Schnee-zwerg' and 'Rubra', euonymus (spindle), and laburnum. Of the last the hybrids 'Vossii' and 'Watereri' are to be avoided as they have few seedpods and so are unlikely to reproduce themselves as desired. *Laburnum vulgare* and *L. alpinum* are the ones to choose and they will look par-ticularly lovely at the top of the quarry or rooting into a ledge above one's head so that one gets the full effect of their dripping golden showers. I do not know whether the garrya would seed itself even if both male and female specimens were grown but the male form of *Garrya ellip-tica* with its long, greeny-grey, suede-like ropes of winter catkins is most effective when planted above a quarry or ledge so that the catkins may droop effectively. The wisteria, too, is excellent for embellishing a quarry face. It may be planted either on the top or bottom and allowed to scramble. A fine effect may also be obtained by planting a wisteria high up and keeping it pruned back to a single short stem of perhaps three feet. The stem will then thicken into a gnarled trunk and the wisteria form an attractive weeping tree. For scrambling upwards the common *Wistaria sinensis* is perhaps the best choice but to trail downwards the long racemes of *W. floribunda macrobotrys* (*multijuga*) in white or lilac are most effective.

*W. venusta* is also fine and very distinctive with downy bronze young shoots and shorter, very thick racemes of white flowers.

Tall genistas such as *Genista aethnensis* and *virgata* are graceful with their late summer shower of golden sparks. These will often seed as will the native brooms of the cytisus section.

Cistus—the large-flowered rock roses of Mediterranean districts—seed freely and succeed on chalk or acid rock. On the dry, sunny ledges of a disused quarry they prove themselves quite hardy. Among the best are: *Cistus* × *corbariensis* with crinkly green leaves and yellow-eyed white flowers, × *cyprius*, the large white flowers of which are boldly blotched with maroon and 'Silver Pink' with silvery grey leaves which effectively set off the pretty pink flowers.

In such a position in full sun, the Judas Tree, *Cercis siliquastrum* is delightful with its heart-shaped blue-green leaves and bright rosy-purple pea flowers borne on the bare wood in May. A white form *C.s. album* is pleasant planted in conjunction with the pink. Rather similar in appeal are the robinias and these may be planted in the sheltered level area at the base of the quarry. One of the prettiest is the soft rose *Robinia hispida rosea* which carries its freely-borne flowers beneath the graceful pinnate leaves of early June. Also good is the new 'Frisia' with bright yellow ferny foliage which lasts through the season to turn coppery before falling in autumn.

An unusual member of the broom family *Cytisus battandieri* will be at its best grown in a pocket at the bottom of the quarry so that it may rear its tall stems, silvery laburnum leaves and fat upright pineapple-scented racemes of tightly packed golden bloom against the rock face.

If the cotoneasters have an authentic folk-name it is that of 'Rockspray'. Certainly nothing is better for covering the bare rocks than *Cotoneaster horizontalis*, the deciduous small-leafed species with scarlet autumn berries that remain after the leaves have crimsoned and dropped. This species presses its arching branch sprays close against the rocks and is immovable in even the worst gale. Like all of its genus, *C. horizontalis* carries in early summer a profusion of single hawthorn-like white flowers that are quite pretty on their own account. Of similar habit, the evergreen *C. microphyllus* may also be used and is useful to clothe the rocks in winter. Its berries though less bright than those of *horizontalis* are nevertheless of a good warm crimson.

On the flatter ground, in the quarry itself, the taller bush-type cotoneasters such as 'Cornubia', *lacteus*, the graceful *salicifolius* and the yellow-fruited × *exburiensis* will all give good winter colour.

The native tutsan, *Hypericum androsaemum*, will seed freely about as will the cotoneasters. Its small but shapely yellow flowers are followed by sprays of berries that turn from green through yellow to red and finally black. All colours are often seen at the same time in one spray with a most attractive effect. More showy in flower though not in fruit, *H. patulum* 'Hidcote' should also be planted. It will make a lightly spreading bush of three or four feet in height and carries large golden 'Rose of Sharon' flowers.

On limestone and chalk, especially, one or two of the clematis species will be rampant enough to hang down over the rocks. In summer and autumn *Clematis orientalis* and *tangutica* will provide a generous curtain of orange or golden bells followed by silvery silky seedheads. Earlier in May, *C. montana* 'Rosea' will veil a generous area with its warm pink stars. In August, *C. flammula* pours down a fragrant mass of hanging creamy panicles not unlike those of the wild 'Traveller's Joy' but sweetly scented.

For winter beauty the trailing *Jasminum nudiflorum*

should be planted above the quarry and allowed to cascade downwards in a shower of lemon beauty.

To cover large areas of rock with beauty or to adorn the walls of ruined buildings, the large-leaved ivies are of the greatest merit. *Hedera colchica dentata* 'Aurea' is a tough, hardy form with large leaves blotched with deep yellow, giving a sunny effect even in winter. *H. canariensis* 'Variegata' is truly lovely, its large leaves shaded in a mixture of cream, grey-green and dark green variegations, sometimes flushed with pink. This last is not a climber for bleak, exposed positions where severe frost will blacken its leaves. The plant itself is seldom even cut back and will throw out fresh leaves in spring so it is worth risking in all but the coldest places. Without variegations but hardy, vigorous and attractive *H. helix* 'Hibernica', the Irish Ivy, has large, bright green leaves and will quickly spread to cover rocks or walls.

For brilliant autumn colour *Parthenocissus* (*Vitis*) *quinquefolia*, the Virginian Creeper is hard to beat. Climbing rapidly and entirely self-supporting it is at its most beautiful when its five-fingered leaves flush first to rose and then to strawberry and finally crimson before they fall. In most districts they persist for some time providing they are not caught too soon by an autumn gale. Even more spectacular hues are attained by the smaller leaves of *P. tricuspidata* 'Veitchii' (*Vitis inconstans*) (*Ampelopsis veitchii*) while those of *P.* (*Vitis*) *henryana* are quietly beautiful all summer with silver and pink veinations against a background of green. To bring out the full beauty of these markings, this species needs to be grown in shade—a north-facing site is ideal.

For a quarry or rock-face *Vitis coignetiae* will form a magnificent feature with its huge leaves, sometimes a foot wide. In autumn these turn to orange and crimson shades of great splendour.

A self-clinging climber of completely different character

is *Schizophragma integrifolia* with good heart-shaped leaves and handsome hydrangea-like lacecap heads with showy single bracts.

Fine to loop itself through the other climbers, *Celastrus scandens* is showy in autumn when its orange-yellow seed capsules split like those of a spindle-tree to show scarlet seeds.

When deciding what smaller plants will seed about to give colour and beauty to the sides of a quarry or the tumble-down walls of an old building one cannot do better than to copy nature. The walls of Conway town in North Wales and the limestone rocks of the Great Orme headland are decorated throughout spring and early summer with yellow and ruby wallflowers. Legend has it that those of the Conway walls originated in the castle garden of Queen Eleanor, wife of Edward I, and that they have seeded down the centuries decorating alike the town and castle walls and the rocks above the quayside walk. The wallflowers of the Great Orme headland can claim no such antiquity; they are escapes from the gardens of houses in the town of Llandudno and on the Marine Drive. In Conway the wallflowers are followed by self-sown antirrhinums. On the rocks of the Orme the succession is taken up by centranthus usually and with botanical inaccuracy known as 'Valerian' or regionally as 'Aunty Betsy' or 'Pretty Betsy' and by the tiny white alyssum of honey-sweet scent.

In Scotland the garden walls of houses that front the road beside Loch Long are starred with purple erinus. This lovely little alpine also jewels the sandstone bridge over the head of Loch Fyne outside Inverary and the high terrace wall of Brodick Castle on Arran. It can readily be established elsewhere. I have had it make itself as much at home on Welsh limestone as in the Scottish sandstone walls. All these wall plants are easy and generous 'doers'. From an original planting of a dozen or two they will seed and spread, finding their own nooks and crannies, high up on top of a ruined wall or on a ledge or crevice in the quarry face.

Some people say they like only the deep red centranthus but I enjoy all colour forms and particularly like to see the crimson, pink and white merging and frothing together against a background of stone blended with the bluey-green of their leaves.

For no other type of garden either wild or conventional would I ever recommend *Cerastium tomentosum*, 'Snow in Summer', because it spreads and seeds so rapidly as to be inclined to take over the whole garden. With a bare quarry to furnish, however, it is to be blessed rather than cursed.

Its white stitchwort-type of flowers are not unpleasing and its mats of silver foliage are neat, if vast, and attractive to the eye. Combined with the autumn leaf colour of the vines already mentioned, cerastium would make a sight of unforgettable splendour.

Efficient carpeters on a lesser scale but rampant enough to give a solid foliage background wherever sufficient soil can be found to start them off, the variegated dead-nettles *Lamium maculatum* and the larger *L. galeobdolon luteum* 'Variegatum' are evergreen and like the cerastium attractive at all seasons.

Gardeners whose homes are among the rocks of a sea-side headland have in the cliffs around them a unique setting for wild gardens of great attraction. Such sea-cliff sites offer, too, fine opportunities for the Parks Departments of seaside towns and boroughs to add to the amenities of their resort. All the perennials and biennials just mentioned will naturalize in such a setting. So too will the Brompton and Ten Day Stocks which have already seeded themselves to become a feature of some Cornish cliffs. The white daisy-flowered *Anthemis cupaniana* with its ferny filigree foliage will also succeed and give an attractive Mediterranean air. Of the shrubs that make themselves at home in such a situation none seed more freely than the rosemary which will make great spreading bushes of aromatic foliage which, so near the sea, become starred with the flowers of misty blue in both autumn and spring. With it, in the south and along the entire west coast of Britain the golden pea-flowered *Coronilla glauca* with its blueish rue-like foliage will bloom from October until May. The shrubby veronicas, *Hebe* species, are useful also for this off-peak period of flower. Indeed it is autumn and winter blooming plants such as these which could help to establish a winter 'season' and help to draw visitors to the milder seaside places. In Llandudno, Deganwy and the Lleyn peninsula of North Wales, for instance, it would be difficult to find a winter's day when some of these plants were not in bloom. *Escallonia macrantha* is another which, in November, December and January, frequently carries numerous sprays of its warm, rosy-crimson flowers.

Of the hebes, it is the varieties of *speciosa* (only really hardy in the shelter of such seaside cliffs) and *elliptica* and their hybrids with flowers of pink, rose, crimson and purple that are most constant in winter bloom. The various forms of *H. salicifolia* will seed freely and make pleasing bushes but their main period of flower is from June to September. The spring-flowering *H. cupressoides* which looks like some dwarf conifer and has a pleasant aromatic scent is another good plant. Of the larger subjects Sea Buckthorn, *Hippophae rhamnoides*, and tamarix can be established where there is a fair depth of soil. Both male and female forms of the Sea Buckthorn must be planted or the brilliant orange berries and consequent seedlings will be absent.

It helps when naturalizing plants on sea-cliffs and other exposed places to make one's initial plantings in the more accessible places to windward of the prevailing wind so that airborne seed may be caught by the wind and carried upwards along the stretch where it is desired to establish the cliff garden. The seed of berry-bearing plants is usually distributed by the birds and so it is best if these are planted on the cliff top or accessible ledges which some small birds haunt. Rock pipits, shore larks, stonechats, chaffinches and wheat-ears among others are found in numbers in such situations on the North Wales coast. Failing distribution by the birds, the berries will eventually rot and the seed drop to lodge in pockets of soil or rock fissures, there to root and grow.

Primroses are not associated in the minds of inland dwellers with sea cliffs, yet shady clefts may often be found, starred with their pale blossoms from top to toe. They may easily be naturalized if planted in such shady gullies or near a cliffside runnel or spring. Thrift, if not already present, may be started on rocks within the spray of the sea and will soon spread. Some of the perennial mesembryanthemums will survive and seed themselves in the milder areas forming evergreen mats starred with their purple and ruby daisies as they do at Criccieth and Abersoch in North Wales and on the sea cliffs of the South-West.

The turf of the cliff top may or may not be carpeted with the pale blue stars of the vernal squill (*Scilla verna*). If not, one may improve upon nature by planting the garden scillas such as *S. sibirica* and *bifolia*. *Chionodoxa luciliae* also will naturalize easily and one might take a lesson from the Scilly islanders and daffodil growers of Cornwall and plant daffodils in sheltered pockets or in the lee of bushes of rosemary and escallonia or clumps of gorse. The dwarf sturdy *Narcissus obvallaris*, the Tenby Daffodil, will be less likely to catch the wind than some of the taller varieties.

In such places one might establish also the Algerian *Iris unguicularis* (*stylosa*) which freely yields its delicately scented lavender flowers from December to March when baked by the sun. The Gladwyn, *Iris foetidissima*, has naturalized itself quite freely in places on the Great Orme headland and is most attractive in late autumn when the seed pods open to reveal the bright orange berries.

A rock plant that makes a good cliff carpeter and spreads rapidly is the golden or lemon flowered *Hypericum patulum* with its small neat leaves and dense, sprawling growth. Good too is the common fennel and this with its lacy yellow flower-heads in late summer is also a good quarry plant.

# CHAPTER SEVEN

# Escarpments, Roads, Spoilheaps, Sandhills ond Forests

FROM moderate excavations carried out in the making of garden terraces, or a tennis court, to the forty- or fifty-foot-high escarpment created by carving new roadways out of hillsides, modern earth-moving equipment often leaves in its wake steep banks the soil of which must be anchored by plant roots if it is not to slip and slide in wet weather. On the garden scale *Hypericum calycinum* can prove an attractive solution with its golden bowl-shaped flowers in late summer, neat evergreen foliage and rapidly spreading habit. Its stems travel under the soil to colonize yet another area, rooting as they go, and it is these roots that help to hold the soil. With it in the garden may be planted the periwinkles and of these the dwarf *Vinca minor* is an even better soil-holder than is *Vinca major*. Plant it closely at nine inches apart and clip it back after flowering to encourage it to bush outwards. As it establishes itself its stems cross and criss-cross, rooting where they touch the ground and binding the bank closely. With the hypericum and periwinkle, variegated ivies such as the little gold splashed *Hedera helix* 'Jubilee Goldheart' or 'Silver Queen' may be planted for contrast, while to give height and summer flowers one might use varieties of the dwarf Scots rose, *Rosa spinosissima*, such as 'Stanwell Perpetual' with its sweetly-scented old-fashioned pale pink flowers, 'Altaica', or the May-blooming yellow *Rosa* × *harisonii.*

When dealing with steep, high escarpments at the side of roadways, however, one must think on an entirely different scale. Drifts of *Hypericum calycinum* and the Scots roses might be used to contrast with larger plants but ivy and periwinkle would be too slow to cover such large areas and at the necessary density of planting would be uneconomic. Shrubs such as *Cotoneaster horizontalis* and the evergreen *C. conspicuus decorus* give continued interest and ground pattern with summer flowers and autumn and winter colour of leaf and berry. The sea-buckthorn and dwarf willows are excellent soil-retainers and have the advantage of spreading well in very poor or sandy soils. Gorse, both the large and the petty whin, are 'naturals' for the job as are the various brooms, particularly the native golden, the creamy *Cytisus praecox*, white *C.p. albus*, and the coloured hybrids. The Rugosa rose varieties will help to give summer colour with white, pink or magenta flowers followed by large tomato-scarlet fruits. These roses are of a spreading-suckering habit and they root deep and wide, helping to bind the soil. The dwarf *Rugosa* 'Max Graf' with single bright pink flowers is a fine plant to use in very steep places. Running widely and rooting frequently, it is one of the best soil-holding plants there is. It is a hybrid between the rugosa rose and the creeping *R. wichuriana.* Good too is *R. paulii* which grows to about four feet with arching, thicketing stems and large crinkled white flowers, gold-centred. For contrast, a plant or two of *R. paulii* 'Rosea' should be included. This form is delightful with pretty clove-scented pink flowers but it is not as vigorous as *paulii.* Another species which will succeed in even the lightest soil is *R. nitida.* Growing only to eighteen inches it spreads widely, thicketing itself with rooting, suckering stems. Its bright pink flowers are followed by showy hips and the leaves colour brilliantly to red in autumn in striking contrast to the ripe corn colour assumed by those of the rugosa section.

On acid soils, the tough native ling can be planted to do the very job that it does so efficiently on many a mountainside, holding back the trickling scree and preventing landslips. It should not be used, however, in places that are too dry. Where the slope is steep and the soil is merely excavated subsoil, lacking the vital humus needed by the ling's fine fibrous roots, gorse will establish more quickly and do a more certain job. On reasonable soils, however, both ling and the Cornish heath, *Erica vagans*, will do well and particularly so in places where there is a down trickle of water from peaty moorland as, for instance, where roadways have been carved through the moors of Scotland and northern England. On limestone the place of the ling may be taken by spreading junipers such as *Juniperus sabina tamariscifolia* and *J.* × *media* 'Pfitzeriana' which though perhaps rather too expensive to plant in quantity are nonetheless ideal to use in small drifts, striking a useful note of contrast in colour and texture with their green, blue-grey and, in the case of *J.* × *media* 'Pfitzeriana Aurea', golden foliage.

Sometimes in the making of roadways it has been possible to use the excavated soil to form landscaped mounds to hide the factories of an outlying industrial belt. Such imaginative use of the excavated soil is worthy of a modern Capability Brown and may well be given the treatment that he would have given it, the mounds being seeded over with grass and crowned with clumps of trees —even mature trees being a possibility thanks to the versatility of present-day machinery which enables specimens of fifteen to twenty feet to be lifted with roots and soil intact, carried for several miles and firmly implanted in their new territory. Where such methods are not available and quick-growing trees are required one might in-

7  *Blechnum tabulare* (*magellanica*) is a handsome fern for sheltered districts. It is hardy in North Wales.

8 The pyracanthas with their foamy-white flowers in spring and fiery autumn and winter berries are striking shrubs for the wild garden and roadside planting.

clude the comparatively new × *Cupressocyparis leylandii* which is hardy and wind-resistant, has elegant grey-green feathery foliage and grows to fourteen feet in a very few years.

The middle strip of dual and treble carriageways presents a different problem offering opportunities to provide plantings that are virtually wild in so much as they need no maintenance and which are restful and visually attractive to the traveller by day; at the same time affording an effective anti-dazzle barrier at night to screen the headlights of the oncoming traffic on one side of the centre-strip from the eyes of the drivers of vehicles which are going in the opposite direction on the other side. If such plantings have the necessary 'give' to act as crash-barriers or catch-nets of living material so much the better.

Excellent plants for the purpose are the taller berberis which form springy thickets of growth. Deciduous varieties such as *Berberis* × *rubrostilla*, *B. vulgaris* and its purple-leafed variety *B.v.* 'Atropurpurea' are ideal. These species carry pleasant yellow flowers among the fresh growth of spring and add large and showy scarlet berries to the fire of autumn foliage. To thicken up the planting and add winter interest, evergreen species such as × *julianae* and × *stenophylla* might be included. Good in milder areas is the laurustinus, *Viburnum tinus* with its pleasant embroidery pattern of star-studded, pink-tinged, off-white flowers against dark evergreen leaves. The heavy ribbed leaves of *V. rhytidophyllum* offer interesting textures and the branches are whippy enough to break the shock of most impacts. Elaeagnus such as the silver leafed *Elaeagnus* × *ebbingei* may also be used. All these will withstand exhaust fumes.

Rose species seldom have sufficiently thicketed growth to be really effective as anti-dazzle agents. The tough rugosas are good value, however, if used among other shrubs such as berberis so that they can add their quota of

F

summer flowers and autumn fruit. To arch above the other growth the tall *Rugosa moyesii* gives interest with its ruby 'Tudor' roses and large bottle-shaped autumn fruits. With its packed lemon flower spikes in early spring, its whippy stems up to five feet or more and its handsome evergreen spiny pinnate leaves, *Mahonia aquifolium undulata* is a fine specimen. Taller and finer than the common *Mahonia aquifolium*, this species suckers freely and will spread to make a dense and attractive planting. Flowering in summer and alas, deciduous, *Tamarix pentandra* with feathery cypress-like foliage and fluffy pink flowers also has the necessary dense growth and whippy stems. It will grow just as well inland as near the sea. *Spiraea* × *arguta* 'Compacta' is an improved form of the favourite 'Foam of May' with hawthorn-like white flowers and a dense springy habit of growth. The later-flowering but rather similar *S.* 'Van Houttei' is also good. Other possibilities are the potentillas and—near the sea—*Hebe salicifolia* and griselinia.

Not only excavations, escarpments and anti-dazzle barriers give the landscape planter chance to make enjoyable roadside plantings. Many of our now-widened roads have spacious verges which would be all the better for attractive naturalistic plantings of shrubs and small trees mingled with wayside flowers. In North Wales various sporadic attempts at such plantings have been made. Some are very successful but—alas—occupy short stretches only. Among the outstanding examples are the orange flowers and neat small holly leaves of *Berberis darwinii* mingled with the narrow grey foliage of sea-buckthorn and topped by laburnum and mountain ash on one of the approach routes to Colwyn Bay and Llandudno. When the rowan berries are ripe those of the berberis resemble bunches of tiny blue grapes and those of the sea-buckthorn glow orange. Farther along the same stretch the dark mounds and golden sprays of *Berberis* × *stenophylla* echo the green spines and yellow bloom of the double gorse, *Ulex europaeus* 'Flore Pleno'. Just over the hedge nearby have been established more sea-buckthorn, and on damper ground the golden barked willow *Salix vitellina* and the feathery deciduous conifer *Taxodium distichum*, the Swamp Cypress, the foliage of which turns to apricot and then russet in autumn.

On another stretch, hardy hybrid rhododendrons mingle with rowans, birch and ferns. Less successful is a planting of picea and abies which, set in isolation, seem to have caught too much wind and many have browned and died. Accidental stretches of bluebells and primroses remain where copses have fallen to the bulldozers and here and there are snowdrops and daffodils which were formerly enclosed by the hedges of cottage gardens. One wonders how long these will be left before being dug up by marauding motorists to join the dying clumps of heather and *Rhododendron ponticum* in their suburban plots. They have been there for three years, however, and have not yet been touched so perhaps there is some hope for the human race. More likely, I fear, they remain because they are growing on a stretch of ground well within sight of several houses and a policeman's cottage!

Despoliation by the country-hungry townsman, however, is more excusable than the despoliation of our wayside flowers by the County Councils with their mobile weed-killer spraying outfits.

In some urban and suburban districts future road-widening plans leave strips of 'no-man's land' between the garden wall or fence and the highway. Speculative builders, too, have in places economized by leaving an unmade strip of earth between the road and narrow pavement. Such plots may be left for years and can be a weedy eyesore. Two methods of dealing with the problem exist— as with roadside verges in the country. One can sow down a strip of grass—and so add to the lawn-mowing chore— or one can plant them with the cheaper shrubs, realizing

that one day they may have to go—but in the meantime
having the enjoyment of them at all seasons of the year.

For such a purpose one might choose the common
*Mahonia aquifolium*, *Aucuba japonica* (the green form
without the spots) planting both male and female to ensure a good crop of scarlet berries, *Forsythia* 'Spectabilis',
ribes and lilac which are extremely easy to raise from
cuttings, mock-oranges, hypericums, potentillas and
buddleias. Tree lupins and brooms will seed themselves.
Such a selection will give colour and interest throughout
the year and with ferns and creeping dead-nettle, *Lamium
maculatum* planted as ground-cover, will help to keep
down weeds.

Spoil-heaps from collieries, slate quarries and other
undertakings in many parts of the country remain unsightly relics often marring attractive districts when with
a little intelligent large-scale wild gardening by the
appropriate authorities they could be transformed into
pleasant rural assets. Many have already been reclaimed
in this way but many more remain.

In time, of course, nature herself will soften the scars.
The seeds of mountain ash and elder will root into the
heap, grass will start to grow and willow herb, nettle and
ragwort will colonize themselves. Man, however, can
hasten the process and try to prevent the ragwort and
nettle invasion by covering the ground first with more
acceptable subjects such as ferns, creeping bugle (*Ajuga
reptans* and *A.r.* 'Atropurpurea'), hypericums (*Hypericum
calycinum* and *androsaemum*), gorse, calluna (ling) and
Cornish heath (*Erica vagans*) on acid soil, foxgloves,
creeping willow (*Salix repens*), the hardy free-seeding
*Hebe brachysiphon* and *elliptica*, *Spiraea* × *arguta*, *thun-
bergii* and *menziesii*, *Berberis darwinii* and the Chinese
hybrids, all of which seed and sucker freely, and the
better snowberries (*Symphoricarpos albus laevigatus*, *S.*
'Magic Berry' and *S.* 'White Hedge'). Of the taller sub-

jects the following will succeed—silver birches, the various rowans (*Sorbus aucuparia* in all its forms along with *S. hupehensis, esserteauiana, matsumurana* and *vilmorinii*), ornamental hawthorns, laburnums and buddleias. Oaks will usually grow on such sites and *Quercus borealis maxima (ruber)* and *Q. coccinea* could be planted for the brilliant scarlet of their autumn leaf colour. Acers of the sycamore type could accompany them. *Acer pseudoplatanus* (pink leaf colour in spring), *A.p.* 'Worlei' (golden) and 'Leopoldii (cream variegated) will usually do well along with the Norway Maple *A. platanoides* in its varieties 'Crimson King' (purple), 'Drummondii' (leaves edged with white) and 'Schwedleri' (purple).

In many seaside areas, sea-defence has made it a necessity to anchor the wind-blown, ever-shifting dunes and to bind them with plant roots. The plants that succeed in such difficult circumstances to meet the need for which they were chosen may—with one or two half-hardy exceptions —be relied upon to do a similar job in difficult soils elsewhere.

Near Newborough Warren on Anglesey, the plantings of the Forestry Commission are helped by various wide-rooting genera that can be relied on to retain the sand. One of the very best of these is the dwarf creeping willow, *Salix repens*, which covers acres of this difficult territory, its roots spreading and holding firmly in little more than pure sand. This little willow grows to about a foot in height with oblong greyish willow-leaves and strong but supple stems. The male and female catkins are borne on separate plants and it is those of the male that are the showiest in late spring when their silky grey fur changes to the bright yellow of ripe pollen. Elsewhere the yellow tree lupin has been planted and has seeded itself freely in shades of gold and cream. White and purple forms of this lupin are also obtainable. Evergreen and sweetly scented, they are delightful subjects to naturalize and when grown in this way seem longer lived, perhaps because they have not received the setback of being transplanted which even when they are set out from pots means that they are exposed to wind-rock before the roots have had a chance to anchor themselves in their new site.

Sea buckthorn, *Hippophae rhamnoides*, will naturalize itself in the same way and in various places along the coast it has been used to hold the sandhills. In North Wales between Deganwy and Llandudno West Shore extensive experimental plantings of this shrub have been most successful. Here, too, the rambling *Lycium chinense* has been used to hold back falling sand. Of no startling beauty, this scrambler makes a pleasant enough patch of green and is good at its job of anchoring the dunes. The variety *L.c. carnosum* is an improvement on the violet-flowered type with pink flowers followed by showy orange or scarlet fruits. *L. halimifolium* (*L. europaeum*) has larger fleshy leaves and is spiny in growth but it is globose in habit and less of a scrambler. It is however quite good to retain the sand or soil.

In this same area of coast the sea-holly grows freely; its extremely long and tenacious roots are equally efficient at binding the sand.

The Scots brier—*Rosa spinosissima*—is found on many patches of coast and both the lowly wild form and the taller selected varieties can be relied on to do a good job of soil retention. One of the best forms, spreading quickly to cover the ground, is the little *R.s.* 'Dunwich Rose' with single, cup-shaped white flowers and a particularly dense habit of growth.

Another species which will grow in almost pure sand is *Rosa rugosa*, large patches of which can be found near Toward Point, Dunoon, in Scotland, at the head of Loch Striven and in many similar wild and exposed localities. Both the white *R.r.* 'Alba' and the magenta pink 'Rubra' will succeed, flowering the summer long and adding showy crops of large, scarlet hips to the golden beauty of their autumn foliage.

In this age vast tracts of country, particularly in North and Mid-Wales and in Scotland, have been afforested and laid down to quick-growing conifers. Some people deplore this but provided some hardwoods such as beech and oak are included to vary the pattern I, myself, do not particularly object. There is something about the resinous scent of the conifer forests with their dark outline and marching rows of tapering trunks that seems suited to our swiftly-flowing rivers, our shadowed lakes and lochs, the sharp outline of the mountains, the circling buzzards and the flash of a russet squirrel among the boughs. The coming of the pines and spruces, the firs and thujas and larches has brought an air of Scandinavian romance to the sometimes grim bare hills. Nevertheless, where the land scheduled for forestry touches the highways, where it comes down to the lakeside, to the river or is crossed by a well-used footpath or rambling route there is a strong case for introducing a few touches of wild-gardening—forest-gardening, as it were, to heighten and pin-point the beauty. That this can be done with very little sacrifice of tree-space and can create memorable patches of beauty has been shown in one or two places in Snowdonia. Along the Capel Curig road to Bettws-y-Coed for instance stands of *Cotoneaster frigidus* hybrids have been planted, their berries in autumn and winter glowing against the rather sombre beauty of the spruces and injecting the scene with warmth and life. Farther on, where a rough track leaves a picnic place for a well-known mountain route, acers and liquidambar have been planted for autumn leaf colour along with rowans and various berried shrubs. The motif could be carried further, of course. The hardier magnolias such as *denudata* and × *soulangeana* 'Lennei', *Davidia involucrata* with its ghost-like bracts, the single-flowered cherries such as *Prunus subhirtella* 'Beni Higan' and *autumnalis* with the graceful blush white *yedoensis*, the rosy 'Okamé' and 'Kursar' might be planted to give a much longer season of interest with such fine viburnums as × *bodnantense*, the spring-flowering *juddii*, followed by *plicatum* var. *tomentosum* with its horizontal tiers of growth and large lacecap flower-heads. Good hardy rhododendrons could be added. The mountain winters would probably be too cold for the large-leafed giants and the early reds of the *arboreum* section but the tough winter-flowering red 'Nobleanum', the May-flowering azalea-like *yunnanense* and the best of the old ironclads such as 'Sappho' with its black-eyed, white flowers, the smoke blue 'Susan', 'Blue Peter' and 'Fastuosum Flore Pleno' would succeed. The Ghent azaleas, too, are extremely hardy; they colour magnificently in autumn and with their honeysuckle-type of flower would not be at all out of keeping with the spirit of the wild. Care should be taken, however, to see that the yellows predominate, toning down and blending together the more strident colours.

For summer interest there are few better subjects than the tall flowering dogwood—*Cornus kousa*—which makes an extremely handsome tree or large shrub. This species is completely hardy and once established carries in June quantities of its large white, elongated star-shaped 'flowers', the apparent 'petals' of which are in fact the pointed bracts surrounding the central cluster of true green flowers. In some years this show is followed by crimson fruits like hanging strawberries. The autumn colour of the leaves is always good with bronze and crimson tones.

In forestry areas with public access it is naturally not practical to use exotic bulbs and plants as underplanting. Moreover, little will grow where the tree-planting is dense. However, primroses can be naturalized on the outskirts, ferns are generally already to be found and foxgloves will grow from scattered seed. Bluebells may be introduced in the same way.

So far as the actual plantings of the trees themselves is concerned much interest can be created by the introduction of different genera—by planting a block of thujas or cypresses among the spruces, by including plantations of larch, both the European and the Japanese species which are so lovely in spring when a purple haze seems to spread over the wood as tufts of red flowers and bursting fresh green needles show on the branches and again in autumn when the needles turn to apricot and russet before falling. The various pines and firs give variety too and when the plantations are planned with care, as in most of the Welsh forests coming under the Forestry Commission's administration, the different shades of foliage appear as a pleasantly patterned rug thrown over the mountain slopes. Even more adventurous plantings might be tried, however. At Crarae in Argyll in the forest garden which Sir George Campbell planted and has given to the Forestry Commission, one of the Southern Beeches—*Nothofagus obliqua* —has proved itself well suited to the climate of North-West Scotland and I am sure that it would do equally well in the very similar climate and soil of North Wales. At Crarae, also, *Abies amabilis*, *A. magnifica* and *A. delavayi* have done particularly well as has *Cryptomeria japonica*. There is a case, too, for planting specimens of such magnificent trees as *Juniperus recurva* var. *coxii*, *Sequoia sempervirens* and the deodars. These might be used to line a ride or forest road or to occupy focal points at the entrance to a planting, or near the picnic-places or viewpoints that the Commission has so thoughtfully provided in many areas, flanked by sorbus species and colourful maples to attract public interest and sympathy to the forestry scheme. One of the Balsam Poplars, *Populus candicans*, might also be included among other hardwoods for the delight of its wonderful scent.

CHAPTER EIGHT

# Naturalization

✣✣✣

NATURALIZATION or the establishing of plants so successfully that they make themselves so much at home as to seed and colonize themselves is one of the most fascinating and important facets of wild gardening. Fortunately, the climate of most parts of Britain is hospitable to many lovely species and the lack of hoeing and 'forking-over' that is part of the policy of wild gardening allows the seeds to germinate and the seedlings to establish themselves and to grow undisturbed.

Various small bulbs are among the best subjects for naturalizing. Of these the early lilac-lavender *Crocus tomasinianus* is well-known as a colonizer. Less well-known, perhaps, but equally successful are the golden *aureus*, the later, larger, lilac-grey *vernus* 'Vanguard' and the newer purple 'Violet Vanguard'.

The common snowdrop will naturalize happily in woodland conditions or along the bank of a hedge, ditch or stream, provided that it is above water level. Dry soil pockets among the rocks of a disused quarry or cliff ledges suit better the southern European *Galanthus elwesii* or *byzantinus*. There is hardly a site in Britain where one species or another of snowdrop cannot be naturalized. It is simply a matter of choosing the one which in nature is found in conditions most closely approximating those of the site of the wild garden in question.

Later flower two species of ornithogalum that seed themselves so freely as to sometimes become a nuisance in the beds and borders of the more conventional parts of the garden. In the wild garden they are always a joy. They are the lowly *Ornithogalum nutans* with upturned chalices of green striped, silvery-grey which flowers in March, and the Star of Bethlehem, *O. umbellatum*, a taller species which carries branching umbels of white flowers with a green stripe in May. The chionodoxas, scillas and blue and white grape hyacinths all lend themselves to naturalizing easily and so do the Greek and Italian anemones. The Greek, *Anemone blanda*, is happiest on a stony ledge where it flowers in March or even earlier with blue or pink daisy-petalled flowers. It needs sun to open fully. On the other hand the Italian *A. apennina* with white or deep blue flowers does very well in shade and is the species to choose for woodland planting. Both spread freely as does the pretty white British windflower (*A. nemorosa*). This species, its double form and the pale blue *A.n.* 'Robinsoniana', the deeper and larger 'Alleni' and 'Blue Bonnet' are all worth planting.

Among the most exciting and challenging colonizers are some of the dwarf species of daffodil. The Lent Lily, *Narcissus pseudo-narcissus* and the Tenby daffodil *N. obvallaris* are easy and will naturalize wherever there is a good depth of soil. The tiny golden *N. cyclamineus* with its long trumpet and reflexed perianth, however, must have a damp peaty soil or it rapidly dies out. It is most likely to establish itself and colonize on the banks of a woodland stream, near a ditch or in a permanently moist but spongy—not waterlogged—patch of ground. *N. bulbocodium*, the Hoop Petticoat Daffodil, on the other hand needs rather drier ground (but not too dry) the short moorland turf of a sunny part of heath garden or the grassy slope above a quarry will suit it admirably. In similar conditions will grow the white 'Angel's Tears' *N.*

*triandrus albus* with its charmingly drooping, reflexed flowers.

Of course, naturalized bulbs spread vegetatively as well as by seed and many of the larger daffodils and narcissi will increase freely in this way. Among those which are particularly satisfactory in the wild garden are 'Carlton', 'John Evelyn', 'Magnificence', 'Flower Carpet', 'Mount Hood' and the old *N. poeticus recurvus* along with such smaller hybrids as 'Peeping Tom', 'March Sunshine', 'February Gold' and 'W. P. Milner'.

With the smaller narcissi the European Dog's Tooth Violet, *Erythronium dens canis* may be interplanted. This species naturalizes well in grass and the rose, white and light purple turncap flowers associate effectively with the primrose and gold of the little daffodils.

Of late the garden bluebells—*Scilla hispanica* (or, more correctly, Endymion) have become rather highly priced. They do increase well, however, and a few dozen will quickly give a stock of the coloured pinks and blues and the large-flowered white that are so pretty in an orchard garden. For the wood, heathland, downland or the waterside, however, the wild bluebells are equally attractive and can be supplied by Messrs. Walter Blom in white and pink as well as blue.

Flowering a little later the sturdy *Camassia quamash* (*esculenta*) bears its wide, pale blue stars on two-foot stems. When it can be obtained the giant *C. cusickii* is even more effective and seeds just as easily in almost any soil.

The only tulip to spread reliably from seed is the late scarlet *Tulipa sprengeri*. Another species, the earlier flowering pretty pink *T. saxatilis*, increases stoloniferously and will quickly form a large free-flowering patch on a sunny ledge of rock or cliff. It is not a species to grow in grass. In such a situation the various gladioli species from South Africa will also thrive. The hardiest and easiest of these are *Gladiolus byzantinus* with magenta flowers, the rose-pink *G. communis*, the rose-purple *G. segetum* and the scented but rather tender cream *G. tristis*. *G. byzantinus* will grow under almost any wild-garden conditions but the others need optimum sun and very good winter drainage.

Not often seen but striking and able to succeed in most gardens the Snake's Head Iris—*Hermodactylus tuberosus*—has narrow green flowers like those of an iris of the Reticulata section and with a vivid purple blotch on the fall. Moist but not wet conditions and full sun suit it best.

The alliums or garlics contain two species—*Allium ursinum*, the native wild garlic and *A. triquetrum* of the Channel Islands and parts of Southern England—which will naturalize all too readily. Some very good gardeners argue that *A. triquetrum* should be admitted as a wild garden plant but it has too much of a garlicy smell for my taste and is no prettier than the white 'bluebell' which at first glance it closely resembles. The golden *A. moly*, however, is worth naturalizing for its sunny umbels and will do well almost anywhere while the rosy *A. cernuum*, the white *A. karatviense* and the lilac *A. albopilosum* do best in a sunny place.

Not often thought of among bulbous species, but actually growing from tubers, the lesser celandine, *Ranunculus ficaria*, will usually come into any wild woodland, orchard or streamside garden whether invited or not and its gold is so welcome in early spring that I, for one, would never oust it. Worth procuring and deliberately introducing is the double form *R.f.* 'Flore Pleno' with perfect rosettes of shining gold, the giant *R.f.* 'Major', the white *R.f.* 'Albus' and 'Primrose' with soft, creamy-yellow cups. These choice forms should really be planted in a near-to-hand part of the wild garden so that an eye can be kept upon them. The hardy cyclamen merit similar preferential treatment. On a sunny quarry ledge or tucked into an old wall the bright carmine *Cyclamen repandum* will succeed. In grass or under trees, except in warm southern gardens, it is not too hardy. Here in North Wales, it is not nearly as easy as *C. neapolitanum*. This species will do well in most districts and will increase by seed. Each individual corm will get bigger, too. Really old corms are soup-plate size and carry more than a hundred flowers. The leaves are handsome. They are shaped like rounded ivy leaves and beautifully chased with silver markings. When they are planted in grass the leaves are hidden, which is a pity. Around the boles of old trees the grass is shorter and the cyclamen find exactly the conditions they like. Their competing growth is thin and one can see and enjoy the beauty of leaves and flowers.

A great deal has been written about the arrangement of bulbs and plants in the wild garden. Most of the advice concurs and may be condensed into two rules. (*A*) Plants and bulbs should be set informally in the way known as 'drift-planting'—that is in ovals of irregular outline rather like cloud formations with one or two outliers a little way off so that they look as if sown by the wind rather than planted by human hand. (*B*) Plant in blocks of a single colour or variety letting it merge gradually into a harmonizing shade or type. For instance, one might begin planting one end of a drift of narcissi with the white 'Mount Hood' then instead of planting next to it a solid gold trumpet such as 'King Alfred' it would be better to plant as intermediary a bi-colour such as the lemon and white 'Spring Glory' and to let it shade to a lemony-yellow such as the large cupped 'Carlton' before reaching the full-toned gold of 'King Alfred'. Similarly with herbaceous plants.

Of herbaceous subjects, the primulas are among the easiest to naturalize. One of the earliest and best is the Drumstick Primula, *Primula denticulata*, which can be obtained in lavender, purple, reddish-purple or white. It will grow in any good soil, either in woodland, at the water's edge or even in the heath garden where it is not too dry. It tends to die out, however, if the soil is too acid so where the pH is below 6 it is advisable to add a little bonemeal or bonfire ash before planting. Another early primula is the small lilac *P. frondosa* with dainty starry flowers on six-inch stems. Both this and the smaller *farinosa* (a native plant of northern Britain) may be established in moist ground or in short downland or mountain turf. Elsewhere they should be planted only at the front of a shrub belt or in a similar place where an eye can be kept on them. They are so small and dainty in growth and in their farinaceous leaves that they might easily be smothered by rank grass or weeds.

Like the Asiatic species suggested for waterside planting, *P. farinosa, frondosa* and *denticulata* will build themselves into clumps and where really suited will seed themselves freely.

Great colonizers, also, are the wild geranium species and some may be found to suit almost any garden situation. For the wild garden generally such species as the tall blue *pratense* with its silver and pink forms, the more compact hybrid 'A. T. Johnson' and the rather similar but yet lower growing *alpinum grandiflorum* are very ready to settle down. So is the raspberry pink *endressii* which not only seeds itself but also hybridizes with any other species that may be in the garden, yielding a variety of plants all rather similar in the neat freshness of their attractively lobed leaves but varying in the height of flower stem and intensity of pink present in their pleasant open flowers. All geranium leaves are redolent of the aromatic 'Oil of Geranium' and none more so than those of *Geranium macrorrhizum* with its bright magenta-pink flowers and those of its white variety *G.m. album*. This latter is a really lovely plant, the white flowers being given a glow of rosy crystal by red stems and calyces. This species seeds itself best in shade. *G. nodosum* on the other hand naturalizes anywhere and is a delightful wild garden plant with smaller flowers of lilac-blue nodding on eighteen-inch stems.

For a quarry garden or similarly dry and stony place *G. ibericum*, the most commonly seen garden cranesbill, will do well. It may be given for company the free-seeding biennial *Salvia turkestanica* with handsome grey leaves and gentle pinky-white bracts, the herbaceous *Phlomis russelliana* with its showy golden-hooded flowers and any of the mulleins (verbascums) which make themselves especially at home on lime.

Getting plants to naturalize well, depends chiefly on choosing them to suit the conditions existing in any particular place. It is useless to try to establish a sun-loving species in dense shade or to persuade plants that need moisture and shade to live on a rock ledge. If plants have the right conditions of climate, soil and aspect they will make themselves at home and spread as they do in nature, forming the large drifts and colonies which are so much more telling in the garden scheme than the spotty effect created by too great a variety of isolated subjects.

Of the geraniums just mentioned, many such as *endressii* and the dark-eyed magenta *psilostemon* (*armenum*) enjoy full sun but there is one—the beautiful, late-flowering *wallichianum* 'Buxton's Blue'—which must have a moist root-run. Plantsmen sometimes eulogize the *subfusc* charms of such species as *phaeum* with tiny, reflexed flowers of dull purple or dark slate, the black-flowered *punctatum* or the dark port-wine *delavayanum*. My personal taste does not run to any of these and I would not recommend anyone to buy them without seeing them. Their foliage is often attractive and I daresay that they have a certain unobtrusive charm, so if you like them, well and good, you may be sure that your choice is in the best of quiet good taste. If not stick to the other species mentioned along with *nepalense*, *sanguineum* (the native

9  *Rosa* × 'Canary Bird' is beautiful in my garden in May. It usually bears a few of its soft, bright yellow flowers again in autumn and the ferny foliage is always good.

10 Rhododendrons and azaleas are among the finest wild-garden subjects for acid soils. 'Letty Edwards' bears her creamy-yellow trusses with us about the middle of May.

Bloody Cranesbill) and its pale pink variety *Geranium sanguineum lancastriense*, the hybrid 'Russell Prichard' with carmine-magenta black-eyed flowers, and the beautiful silver-leafed *renardii* which is particularly effective on a rock-ledge or stony slope.

Columbines (aquilegias) are among some of the best colonizers. Here the question is not how to get the plants to increase but how to prevent poor forms creeping in and predominating. To this end only good strains should be introduced in the first instance. Miss Jekyll's 'Munstead White", Mrs. Scott-Elliott's strain of long-spurred hybrids, and species such as *Aquilegia canadensis* with a good form of the blue *alpinum* should give rise to a pleasing mixture. Even so, specimens of the old 'Granny's Bonnet' type of ugly form and dull colours may occur—or even the stumpy doubled varieties—and these should be ruthlessly pulled up and burned before they seed or contaminate the others by pollen that might perpetuate undesirable characteristics.

Another genus valuable to the wild gardener is that of campanula. Again there are species to suit all situations. For the cliff or quarry site the trailing rampant *Campanula poscharskyana* is a boon, festooning and draping rock faces with its pale violet-blue stars. More compact but hearty, pretty, and almost equally ready to colonize is *C. portenschlagiana* (*muralis*) with deep hyacinth-purple harebells. For orchard, woodland or to naturalize in grass the taller species such as the white and blue forms of *persicifolia*, *lactiflora* and the purple wildling *glomerata* are ideal.

Violets naturalize readily in cool woodland conditions and in addition to the scentless dog violet, which is by no means to be despised as ground cover, one can often establish the scented *Viola odorata* forms in white, creamy-ivory, sulphur (*V. sulphurea*), sky blue ('John Raddenbury'), large purple ('Princess of Wales'), pink ('Coeur d'Alsace') and wine ('Red Queen' or 'St. Anne's Red').

G

When happy these will seed and intermingle, yielding a varied crop of delight. The scentless but showy white and purple *V. septentrionalis* also is usually easily established, while some of the larger viola species still retain a wildling grace and are not out of keeping in sunnier, stony places. Of these the native *lutea* spreads even in pure sand and makes a pattern of pansy faces varying from yellow and ivory to purple, mauve and plum-red. Some are self-coloured and some bi-colours, often whiskered and mottled in fascinating array. Pretty and graceful, too, are the larger flowers of *V. cornuta* in shades of blue, near-black and a velvety white. There is also *V. labradorica* which is more like a dog violet but with slightly larger, purple flowers and pleasing plum-coloured foliage.

Nor is the common Forget-me-Not to be despised. Sowing itself freely it will form wide drifts and colonies, misting the grass with its tender hue or complementing the rose, flame or yellow of azaleas with its soft tint of the summer sky.

Some of the pulmonarias seed freely. People are apt to be critical of the lush spotted leaves of the type *Pulmonaria officinalis*, 'Soldiers and Sailors'. This is an attitude that I cannot understand. The species *saccharata* has more handsome leaves than the type but all are attractive with large blueish-white spots on the softly hairy green leaves. Spreading as they do they make invaluable ground cover in the wild garden. On the other hand they never become seriously invasive. The flowers, too, are pretty—pink and blue and carried in crozier heads. Another species, *P. angustifolia*, has narrow unspotted leaves and bright gentian blue flowers that appear a little later than those of *officinalis* and *saccharata* which are usually out by March. *P. rubra* also has narrow leaves. Its flowers are salmon-red and it is usually the first species to flower, as early as February if the weather is mild.

The pulmonarias belong to the borage family as do the

anchusas. I have found the summer-flowering tall *Anchusa italica* with its gentian blue flowers to naturalize well. The tall stems flop but this does not seem to matter. With half the stem prostrate, the end turns upwards giving flowers for a foot or eighteen inches above ground while the prostrate parts of the stems and the hairy leaves act as weed suppressors. More of a conventional wild garden plant is that which used to be known as *A. myosotidiflora* now removed to a different genus and labelled *Brunnera macrophylla*. Seeding itself to produce solid drifts its large summer leaves make excellent ground-cover and the tiny bright blue flowers are generously borne on widely branching sprays from May to July. Also blue-flowered, *Polemonium caeruleum* (Jacob's Ladder) is an old cottage garden plant that flowers in summer and seeds widely to make attractive clumps of ladder-like ferny leaves. The nodding flowers carried on eighteen-inch stems are harebell-blue with a golden centre.

Foxgloves and mulleins are among the best plants for colonizing. Both tall and stately, the foxglove grows most freely in woodland or in heath. It is on limestone ground and in sunny places that the mulleins (verbascums) are to be found. Among the finest of these are *Verbascum chaixii* (*vernale*), a good perennial with large grey-green leaves and five-foot candelabras of yellow spikes from June to August. *V. olympicum* has even more handsome leaves, large and silver-felted, while its gold spikes may reach to six feet in height. Also good is the biennial *V. bombyciferum* (broussa) with silver basal rosettes and woolly grey spikes carrying the bright gold flowers to five feet. It may be relied upon to renew itself generously from seed.

To my mind it is this happy seeding of plants to form colonies with odd outliers that is the main theme of the wild garden. The recurrence of a species throughout the garden is a unifying note. One of the most cheerful and accommodating self-seeders is a biennial evening primrose—*Oenothera lamarckiana*, with tall spikes carrying quite large golden flowers that mainly open in the evening. They are nostalgically scented and are borne along the side shoots too. This species will flower and increase almost anywhere.

Catmint, *Nepeta* × *faassenii* (*mussinii*) is another free-seeding plant and is particularly good for rocky outcrops, quarry gardens, old walls and cliffs where it will blend with the 'valerian' to form an attractive colour combination.

Numbers of shrubs will, where they are happy, seed themselves in this obliging fashion. Of these none are more prolific than the brooms. Near the sea, rosemary will often seed itself almost as freely and on peaty soil and even in woodland baby heaths will often be found if there is any heather or ling in the vicinity. Cotoneasters, too, reproduce themselves in this way, usually choosing the most picturesque sites. Rose species are ready seeders, sometimes giving rise to valuable and most decorative offspring. The tall-growing *Rosa moyesii* is one of the most apt to reproduce itself like this and so, indeed, are the burnets (*spinosissima*) and the sweetbriars. Hypericums often seed freely and are usually very welcome with their golden, bowl-shaped flowers and graceful habit; so are the potentillas, sea-buckthorn and berberis of which *darwinii* is one of the most persistent colonizers that I know. In well-drained, sunny places cistuses and buddleias appear in quantity from self-sown seed and so does the pretty *Coronilla glauca* with its rue-like leaves and golden yellow broom-flowers that are so welcome in winter. Other shrubs that seed themselves are laurustinus, hebe, holly, leycesteria, *Laburnum anagyroides* and, to a lesser extent, daphne, while among the most pleasant surprises I have known was the appearance in quantity of small seedlings of evergreen azaleas, deciduous azaleas and the small-leafed rhododendrons in the moss of a woodland glade. I have found also seedlings of halesia—one of the attractive snowdrop trees, various maples (acer), wild cherry, birch, fuchsia, pyracantha, *enkianthus* and euonymus.

Some of these may be growing in unsuitable positions and will need resiting when they are big enough to move safely. Others may stay where they are and will often do superlatively well in their self-chosen sites.

Other plants colonize by running roots or by suckers: most of these come into the category of ground cover and so will be dealt with in the next chapter. One lovely shrub which spreads in this way but is not close enough in growth to be counted as ground cover is the tall *Romneya coulteri* with gold-bossed, large crinkled, silky white poppy-flowers. It needs a sunny, well-drained site.

# CHAPTER NINE

# Ground Cover

SUCCESSFUL wild gardening depends in part on the use of plants to cover the bare earth and so keep down the weeds, working on the knowledge that weeds need light to germinate. One has only to think of the sparse plant life on the floor of a thickly-planted spruce forest to realize the truth of this.

Grass is one of the most effective carpeters of all and is used extensively in orchard gardens and in the more open type of wild garden. In other places one might use a carpet of heaths—shearing the plants after flowering to keep the growth dense and to prevent light from reaching the soil beneath. A solid matt of foliage three to four inches deep will effectively prevent weed germination. Weeds are also prevented from developing where a close mat of roots exists, denying them all room. Astilbes and wood-rush (luzula) work in this way. Wood-rush is one of the most attractive ground covers for woodland use and will effectively suppress all weeds. Such an efficient carpet, of course, also suppresses bluebells, wood anemones and primroses, so it must be kept to the rougher parts where weeds and brambles might otherwise be a serious problem. Its growth is too dense for it to be used under young shrubs although it will not harm established trees.

One of the best carpeters of all for woodland floor is the

ivy which may already be found to be growing there. Suppressing most coarse weeds—but not, alas, brambles —it yet allows snowdrops, bluebells, hardy cyclamen and other treasures to spear through. Primroses nestle in it. A combined carpet of ivy and the blue dwarf periwinkle *Vinca minor* 'Atrocaerulea' with wild dwarf daffodils pushing through is one of the most exciting wild garden sights. Periwinkle alone is quite satisfactory—providing it is clipped over after its spring flowering to keep the growth dense. The blue, white and claret varieties whether double or single are all equally effective.

Ivy is often slow to spread. Not unnaturally the large-leafed species *Hedera colchica* in both plain and variegated forms is the quickest to cover the ground. A bi-generic hybrid × *Fatshedera lizei* with large ivy-shaped leaves is even quicker to spread.

For poor soil or good, a dwarf comfrey, *Symphytum grandiflorum*, is one of the best weed suppressors. It makes dense carpets of rough green leaves and in spring and autumn sends up six-inch croziers of creamy, orange-tipped bells. Under its country name of 'Cherubim and Seraphim' it is beloved of cottagers everywhere. A relative of the comfreys, *Trachystemon orientalis* is a much taller plant and one of the quickest spreading non-weedy subjects that I know. Anywhere but in the fairly extensive wild garden its outsize rosettes of soft, hairy grey-green leaves would be a nuisance. Where weed-suppression is to be done, however, it is a boon and its soft-blue flowers on eighteen-inch stems are pretty and welcome in spring.

Dwarfer in habit but none the less dense and most efficient at its job of weed suppression is another member of the borage family, *Borago laxiflora*, with green hairy leaves and lax stems of decorative turquoise flowers like little pointed bells. It has a very fast rate of spread and also naturalizes itself by seed as does the trachystemon. I like to plant with it the copper-leafed bugle, *Ajuga reptans*

'Atropurpurea'. Both do well in sun or shade and are good to cover sloping banks. In shade, the copper-leafed bugle may be used with a softly variegated variety of the same species *A.r.* 'Multicoloralis' ('Rainbow') or with the tortoiseshell-marked *A.r.* 'Metallica'.

In woodland, good weed-suppression may be obtained with the Lenten roses, *Helleborus orientalis* hybrids, set at eighteen inches apart and allowed to seed as they will freely do. It will take most of their offspring three years to flower from seed although a few can be relied on to flower in their second year. When planted in a drift, nothing will grow under the spread of the Lenten roses' handsome palmate leaves. Their flowers are attractive, drooping, speckled bowls of greeny-white, apple-blossom, peach-blossom, claret and matt dove-purple. Contrary to an often repeated misbelief by those who do not know the trick, they are fine for cutting provided that their stems are split up the middle for three to four inches before being plunged to the neck in warm water. The native *H. foetidus* has large, graceful bunches of small apple-green cups that are rimmed with prune-purple as they age and is a good plant to use for ground cover.

Two liliaceous plants—Lily of the Valley (*Convallaria majalis*) and Solomon's Seal (*Polygonatum multiflorum*) are effective in weed suppression making a solid mat of rootstocks and leaving the soil so drained of moisture and nourishment that nothing else can grow. Both, of course, are well-loved and attractive plants in their own right. They will naturalize extensively and add considerably to the charm of a woodland garden.

Good, too, but quite different in character are dwarf shrubs such as *Gaultheria procumbens* with neat dark little leaves and white heath-like flowers followed by bright red berries in winter. The taller *G. shallon* is effective, too, but much taller in growth. It grows to three feet or more in height and is thicket forming. Its pale pink flowers are

followed by dark red fruits. Both gaultherias are evergreen. The rather similar vacciniums of which our native
bilberry is a representative are mainly deciduous but they
are none the less efficient at keeping down the weeds. I
have used wild bilberries for this purpose and the cran-
berries *Vaccinium macrocarpum* and *V. oxycoccus* may also
be grown. The American blueberry *V. corymbosum* is taller
in growth like *Gaultheria shallon*. All are worth planting
and it is pleasant to have the added enjoyment of their
fruits. They are as good on heathland as in the wood
although where native heath and ling exist it is as well to
let them carry out their natural role.

Plants vary greatly in their efficacy as weed-smother
but all those I have mentioned here can be relied upon to
do their job. To give them a fair chance a light hoeing
should be carried out twice-yearly for the first year or two
until the leaves have touched and joined up into a dense
carpet of foliage.

Another ground-covering subject that I have found
useful, especially in poor dry soils, is *Cynoglossum nervosum*,
the Chinese Hound's Tongue with dark-green hairy
foliage and bright blue forget-me-not flowers over the
whole of the summer and often into the winter as well. It
does not make a brilliant colour splash as there is more
expanse of leaf and stem than flower area but it has charm
and it is a superb weed-suppressor, succeeding even in
gravel or shingle or among the rubble at a quarry base.

I have written earlier about the variegated dead-nettles
but I must mention them again here because their in-
terestingly patterned leaves make a carpet so dense that
weeds seem never to push through and they will succeed
anywhere—in sun or shade. *Lamium maculatum* is prostrate with small soft green leaves splashed with silver that
in the winter take on a tinge of pink. *L. galeobdolon
luteum* 'Variegatum' has larger leaves marked with silver
and will make a taller plant with Yellow Archangel

flowers. It is fine to cover a stony bank and used in wood-land to clothe the dry, rooty ground under trees it is magnificent, its foliage seeming to catch the light and making a river of silver and soft green.

Very good, too, is the old-fashioned *L. orvala* with leaves of soft plain green and hooded flowers of red or white. Like a very superior dead-nettle it is unfortunately not readily obtainable today but it suppresses weeds so efficiently all spring and summer and is such a charming plant that I think a determined effort should be made to reintroduce it and to popularize it.

To clothe a difficult bank is one of the chief functions of *Hypericum calycinum* (Rose of Sharon). It makes a pleasant cover of shapely, soft-green, matt-surfaced leaves and its golden flowers are handsome. I have never known its territory to be invaded by a single weed but to make absolutely sure of its efficiency it may be sheared over after flowering to keep it neat and compact.

Some of the most useful geranium species were described in the last chapter. Those which I have found to be the most efficient as ground cover in almost any conditions are the pink *Geranium endressi*, *G.* 'A. T. Johnson' with its salvers of cornflower blue, *G. ibericum platyphyllum, macrorrhizum* in its various forms, 'Russell Prichard' and *renardii*. With fairly long flowering spells, fragrant leaves and attractive blooms, they are all good garden value.

Some of the polygonums are rampant weeds on their own account but there are several more restrained species which are valuable as ground cover in the wild garden. Least vigorous of these but making good mats of pleasant foliage that colours to red in autumn is *Polygonum vaccinifolium* with heath-like spikes of pure pink flowers. It is good to plant in the forefront of heaths or to grow among rocks. Moreover, if one looks on a wild garden as something more than a piece of rough ground to be gardened

in the easiest possible way and rather as one of the most
satisfying and lovely parts of the garden one may include
a few treasures and plant this polygonum in conjunction
with the graceful willow-leafed gentian *Gentiana asclepiadea*
or with the dwarfer easy Asiatic hybrid, *G. macaulayi* in a
reasonably moist or peaty place.

A good form of the native Bistort, *P. bistorta* 'Superbum' though not such a choice plant as *P. vaccinifolium*, is pleasing for much of the year and will spread to
give effective ground smother. Its fat little spikes of pink
rear above dock-like leaves of fresh green. Similar but not
as reliably hardy in cold districts is the Indian species *P.
affine* from Nepal with dense narrowly pointed leaves and
flowers of a rosy pink. There is also a crimson-flowered
form known as 'Darjeeling Red' which makes a good contrast but does not increase as quickly. The leaves of both
turn to an attractive fox-russet which persists through the
winter. These two species will grow in sun or shade. The
bistort will do well even at the streamside but in cold
districts *P. affine* will be more trustworthy in a sunny,
stony place.

In such a place, too, *Stachys macrantha* (*grandiflora*)
(*Betonica*) is useful, spreading itself thickly to keep down
weeds. From its big heart-shaped, downy leaves rise
fifteen-inch stems carrying whorls of hooded mauve
flowers. It is a handsome old-fashioned plant—good to
use for contrast in the foreground of heathland or at the
foot of a quarry or wall, wherever there is enough soil to
support it. Preferring rather damper ground but able to
spread well in any reasonable loam is the Self Heal,
*Prunella grandiflora*, in its garden varieties of lavender,
rose and white. In too dry a place its growth is not sufficiently dense and weeds creep in but wherever the soil is
good the prunella will form a most effective smother and
its pretty hooded flowers are cool and delightful to come
upon.

For drier ground, two garden herbs do good service as weed suppressors. They are the bright little golden-leafed marjoram, *Origanum vulgare* 'Aureum' and the variegated horehound *Marrubium vulgare* 'Variegatum' with soft grey-green leaves thinly splashed with cream. They combine well with the Chinese Hound's Tongue, *Cynoglossum nervosum*, mentioned earlier in this chapter.

The yellow Loosestrife, *Lysimachia punctata*, with its spikes of quite large, wide-open treacle-gold flowers is a fine ground cover in moist soil or dry, its roots matting thickly to keep down weeds. Less well-known is its relation *L. clethroides* which prefers a moist position. It carries a thick spike of white flowers in a long buddleia-like spike, nodding at the top in a gentle curve.

The genus *Epimedium* provides several first-class weed suppressors among its species. All have pretty leaves that in autumn are tinted with crimson, russet and gold and are carried on long wiry stalks. The flowers like tiny columbines in yellow, rose, crimson and white are carried in airy sprays in spring. Often the winter-browned leaves tend to obscure the flowers. Some people remove the foliage to show up the flowers but if this is done too soon the blooms may be frosted. Also the clumps will look tatty until the new leaves grow but the clumps are too dense for the cutting of the foliage to interfere with its effectiveness as weed smother. However, I prefer to let most of the leaves remain and to content myself with picking some of the flower sprays for the house where they look pretty with a few of their own leaves in a small jug of polished pewter.

Perhaps the epimediums prefer a cool soil but they will grow almost anywhere and steadily creep to form densely handsome drifts of ground cover. One or two species are not really robust enough as carpeters for the wild garden but among the prettiest and most efficient are *E. grandiflorum* 'Rose Queen', *perralderianum* with large glossy leaves and yellow flowers, × *versicolor* 'Neo-sulphureum' and × *warleyense* with orange flowers. The pretty white-flowered × *youngianum* 'Niveum' is much smaller and more slow to increase. It is best to use in a more cultivated part of the garden as are the rosy-mauve *E.y.* 'Roseum' and × *rubrum* with dainty white-spurred crimson flowers.

Equally attractive, *Cornus canadensis* is a plant strictly for lime-free soil. Spreading rapidly in woodland soil or sandy heathland peat this creeping Dogwood forms rosettes of ribbed leaves crowned in June by a typically handsome white Dogwood flowers which are later followed by red berries.

As easy as the epimediums is *Tiarella cordifolia*, the Foam Flower of North America. The tiarella is pretty in spring with its six-inch spires of fluffy cream flowers and its lobed heart-shaped leaves that become tinted with crimson in the autumn. With a running rootstock it spreads well and forms a dense mass of foliage.

Not dissimilar, *Tellima grandiflora* is a taller plant with rounded hairy leaves and two-foot spikes of pale green fringed bells. There is a valuable purple-leafed form of this, *T. g.* 'Purpurea' with yellowish flowers.

Another American which has enjoyed a surge of popularity recently is the pachysandra but I think this is too dull and characterless for British wild gardens where climatic conditions are so much easier than in most parts of the U.S.A. and where so many more attractive alternatives therefore exist. Among these alternatives is the intriguing 'mouse-plant', *Arisarum proboscideum*, which forms low clumps of dark green spear-shaped glossy leaves amid which nestle the quaint little long-tailed arum flowers for all the world like purplish-grey mice. A true arum, *Arum italicum marmoratum* produces ordinary green 'Lords and Ladies' flowers in October followed by beautiful leaves, marbled with grey, green, white and yellow which last the winter. Less noticeably blotched but with

the veins picked out in creamy yellow is another winter
joy, the handsome *A. italicum pictum*. These last three
plants are by no means rapid carpeters but rather small
treasures of the sort without which no wild garden is
complete.

In woodland or on heathland or downland, the common
holly-leafed berberis, *Mahonia aquifolium* makes good
ground cover. Spreading by its running rootstocks it will
form dense undulating drifts with its handsome compound, spiny leaves and fat, bright yellow flower spikes in
March. In sunny places they often turn to bronze in
autumn. There is also a form *M.a.* 'Atropurpurea', the
leaves of which are purple for most of the year.

Bergenias and hostas are often referred to as ground-
cover plants but I do not think bergenias are really in
keeping in the wild garden. Many people will not agree
with me, I know, but to my mind they strike too formal a
note. Hostas on the other hand are lovely in woodland but
I think of them as plants for special emphasis rather than
as efficient ground cover. *Alchemilla mollis*, the Lady's
Mantle, is at home anywhere and looks it. Its beautiful
grey-green rounded leaves are covered with silky down
and are dense enough to make it a really good weed-
suppressing plant. In summer masses of tiny greeny-yellow
starry flowers are carried in airy spray. Seeding freely it
will naturalize, spreading to make a wide carpet of lovely
foliage.

For a quarry garden, cliff or similar sunny, well-drained
position some of the artemisias are good with silvery
foliage that seems to fit in with the sun-baked character of
the setting. One of the best is the lowly *A. canescens* with
lacy but dense filigree foliage. Taller, *A. ludoviciana* make
a good contrast with its four-foot stems of grey-white
willow leaves. Its roots run to form a thicket. Lower
again in growth, *A. pontica* is a rapid and dense colonizer
with pretty sprays of feathery grey-green foliage. In a

similar position some of the pinks will naturalize well and their close mats of grey, grassy leaves make dense ground cover. Apart from *Dianthus gratianopolitanus* (caesius) the native Cheddar pink, the 'Highland Hybrids' and 'Allwoodii Alpinus' will quickly colonize from self-sown seed. I have never known the South African *Dimorphotheca barberiae* to seed itself but it is a fine ground-covering plant for full sun and sharp drainage. Making wide patches of tufted, rounded leaves its pretty lilac-pink daisies are carried on six- to nine-inch stalks from May often until December. On seaside cliffs, *Felicia pappei* var. *gracilis* (*Aster pappei*) with smaller but vivid sky-blue daisies and dense tufts of bright green, narrow leaves will usually survive the winter and is so easily raised from cuttings that it is well worth the risk. On the south and west coasts at least it is long lived and will sometimes seed itself. Within a few feet of the sea and the influence of the Gulf Stream it would take a winter such as 1962–63 to do it harm.

To make efficient ground cover many of the plants mentioned should be set at a foot to eighteen inches or two feet apart. On a big scale their use would be expensive so it is best to progress gradually, taming a little more of the wild each year but always using those plants that are so much in character with their surroundings that they blend with them looking as if they came there naturally. One false note such as the introduction of a garish or unsuitable plant and the effect of the wild garden can be ruined.

By purchasing a few plants of the desired species and propagating by stem or root cuttings or by layers or by taking rooted suckers one can quite quickly build up a good stock. Many plants can also be raised from seed. Indeed, with the various primula and geranium species, the mulleins, foxgloves and other herbaceous subjects this is often the quickest way of obtaining a large stock. One cannot rely, of course, on the seed always breeding true; accidental hybridization may have occurred, but in the wild garden this is not usually a serious matter. One keeps the pleasing forms and discards the rest. Some bulbs can be naturalized from seed. Bluebell seed scattered in orchard or woodland will usually result in success. Snowdrop seed pods buried green will result in new plants. The dwarf narcissi and American erythronium species come freely from seed sown in a moist or peaty place.

Many creeping weed-suppressors can be readily pulled to pieces to make new plants. If each piece is inserted separately at six inches apart they will quickly spread to form a mat. *Lamium maculatum*, *Ajuga reptans*, Solomon's Seal, pernettya, prunella, epimediums, *Marrubium vulgare* 'Variegatum', *Symphytum grandiflorum*, *Lysimachia punctata*, mimulus species, astilbes, tiarella, *Cornus canadensis*, irises of the *sibirica*, *chrysographes* and *ochroleuca* type and *Borago laxiflora* can all be increased in this way as can the day lilies—useful and ornamental plants in their own right and good weed suppressors.

Primulas, lysichitums, cynoglossum, anchusa, *Trachystemon orientalis*, oriental poppies, dicentra and many plants with thick fleshy rootstocks can be readily propagated from root-cuttings; pieces of root about an inch long being inserted in a box of compost of sand and peat in spring, covered with polythene or with a glass and left to sprout.

Heaths strike readily from cuttings of side shoots half an inch to one inch long insrted in pans of peat/sand (3 : 2) compost in late August, kept close until rooting has taken place and then gradually hardened off until finally the frame lights can be removed. Dwarf rhododendrons, azaleas, gaultherias and *Polygonum vaccinifolium* may be increased in the same way.

Thicket-forming shrubs such as *Viburnum fragrans*, and × *bodnantense*, *Stephanandra tanakae*, many spiraeas and the attractive Russian dwarf almond *Prunus tenella* (*nana*) with its small deep pink flowers may be divided and have

12  Purists may not agree but I think the round-headed blue varieties of *Hydrangea macrophylla* are perfectly in keeping in the wild. Here they have orange crocosmia (montbretia) as companions.

suckers removed to start new colonies. The useful hardy geranium species and most other herbaceous plants may be divided readily.

Many rose species and some climbers such as winter- and summer-flowering jasmines, the ivies and vines may be pegged down to form rooted layers. The periwinkles also may be increased in this fashion, a shovelful of earth thrown over their long trailing stems will encourage them to root along their length. The rooted pieces may then be severed from the parent to form new plants.

Many hardy shrubs such as the mock orange, weigela, flowering currant, kolkwitzia, forsythia, elaeagnus and many roses may be rooted by taking a long shoot with a heel and inserting it well into the ground in October or early spring. The more tender lavenders, cistus, rose-maries and senecio are best struck in spring.

H

# CHAPTER TEN

# A Wild Corner and Garden Treasures

WILD gardening is a fascinating conception, tantalizing to those of us with ready-made gardens. Yet even in the smallest suburban plot the pleasures of the wild need not be wholly denied.

A garden in grass may be planted around the bole of an established tree. On the lawn of our former garden we left two boat-shaped areas of rough grass under a 'Cheal's Weeping Cherry'—the rosy, very double-flowered variety —and under the pink winter cherry, *Prunus subhirtella autumnalis* 'Rosea'. In the grass were snowdrops followed by a number of *Crocus chrysanthus* forms in yellow, yellow striped with brown, marigold-centred cream, white shaded with violet and some pretty blues. These were succeeded by the grey-lavender *tomasinianus* the larger similarly coloured *vernus* 'Vanguard' and purple, white and striped forms of the fat Dutch hybrids. Two little wild daffodils followed in late March and April, the golden trumpeted *Narcissus obvallaris*, the Tenby daffodil, and the pale Lent Lily, *Narcissus pseudo-narcissus*. The pink and blue lungwort, 'Soldiers and Sailors'—*Pulmonaria officinalis*—accompanied them along with primroses and later cowslips. Then came the early purple orchid— *Orchis mascula*, the chequered and white bells of the fritillaries and in late May the tall stems of *Camassia quamash* (*esculenta*) with its pale blue stars. At the end of June the grass was rough cut. It was cut again in August to leave the way clear for the rosy-lilac chalices of the colchicums, like large crocuses, which in autumn foretell the spring.

Beneath older trees where the grass is sparse or non-existent one might plant in addition the tiny wild cyclamen, the autumn *neapolitanum* in white or pink with shapely, silver-patterned leaves that make a wonderful ground work for the rounder blossoms of the winter-flowering *orbiculatum* and its variety *coum*.

Or one might start a wild garden from scratch, as it were, by planting a group of silver birches—from three to five is ideal—or in a very small garden one might plant instead a single specimen of 'Young's Weeping Birch', *Betula pendula* 'Youngii'. Rough grass (Turk-scythed twice or three times a year) ferns and a clump or two of mahonia with spring bulbs completed the setting. Bluebells might be added with foxgloves for later summer. Several excellent strains of foxglove exist. One seed firm offers seed of separate colours—apricot, white and yellow. The 'Shirley' strain too is good with wide, generously spotted bells in rose, pink and white.

Campanulas look well amid the grass in a wild corner and for this purpose, I use *Campanula persicifolia*, seed raised, in blue and white.

An uncommon and lovely wild garden for grass is chicory (succory) with its blue, daisy-like flowers of soft sky blue. This stars the grass with great effect in the grounds of the Lloyd George Museum at Dwyfor, near Criccieth in Caernarvonshire. It, too, may be raised from seed and an extra bonus will be won if one sows more than one needs for the wild garden. The surplus plants are taken up in autumn, their older leaves removed and the roots shortened. They are then planted in the dark;

under a box beneath the greenhouse bench or in a cellar is ideal, or they may simply be potted, placed in a shed or garage and covered with an upturned box or bucket to yield blanched leaves for the delicious winter salad which the French call 'Barbe de Capucin'.

Where a garden is larger than the owner would wish, making more demands than time or strength allow, the problem may most happily be solved by grassing down the unwanted area, planting bushes, apple trees or birches and naturalizing bulbs and meadow flowers such as trollius and columbine, cowslip and cow-parsley, therein. Ready-made wild garden opportunities exist wherever there is a grassy hedge-bank, particularly if a ditch is present. In the grass primroses and violets, snowdrops, aconites, hellebores and the smaller daffodils will establish themselves readily and make a colourful tapestry for spring. With them may be associated the dwarf periwinkles in blue, white and claret. The delightful larger-leafed *Vinca major* 'Elegantissima' may also be grown and will yield graceful trails of cream-splashed foliage. Cream and golden variegations of *Vinca minor* also exist and will help to add charm and variety. As spring gives way to summer, bluebells will mist the bank with their hyacinth haze. With them one may invite the white campion to naturalize. Often the pink campion comes of its own accord but I think its tone is too harsh for the bluebells and the white should be grown instead.

If the bank is shady and reasonably moist the American *Trillium grandiflorum* will do well as it does in woodland. With its large white, three-cornered flowers backed by three large deeply veined green leaves it is not surprising that it is also known as the Trinity Flower. Where it succeeds the early purple *Orchis mascula* will usually grow as will the Madeiran *O. foliosa* with massive spikes of purple-mauve flowerlets. At a guinea or more a plant, however, this is too expensive a treasure for most of us.

The Lady's Slipper Orchid *Cypripedium calceolus* is less expensive and quite lovely with its quaintly pouched 'slippers' in yellow and brown. It will grow in such a place as this if the soil is not too acid and if it is generously supplied with leaf-mould on planting and later given topdressings of the same. The American *C. reginae* may sometimes be obtained and is reasonably easy in a cool leaf-mould packed soil. It will tolerate a more acid medium.

Queen Anne's Lace and foxgloves may be used to follow on and in autumn the colchicums will take up the tale. Ferns and the Italian *Arum italicum pictum* may be used to complete the picture. Even the hedgerow itself may be incorporated into the wild garden with *Clematis montana* to flower in spring and the hermaphroditic form of *Celastrus orbiculatus* to drape its spindle-like fruits over the colouring leaves in autumn. The Penzance hybrid sweetbriars too might be incorporated if room can be found to set them close against the hedge so that they may intertwine and mingle in a natural way.

Cornish 'hedges' which are really stone walls with a hedge on top may be similarly treated being cleansed of nettles and coarse weeds before planting. Some people strip the grass from their Cornish 'hedges' but this, I think, is a pity. Not only does it weaken the structure by removing the grass roots which help to bind the soil doing duty as a mortar but the grass if kept in trim provides a pleasant background for the flowers.

Where there is a ditch at the foot of the hedge one may grow simple marsh flowers such as the kingcup and the yellow globe trollius with water-avens, *Primula denticulata* and the later candelabras, *Iris chrysographes* and *sibirica* and the large-flowered *I. kaempferi* which bloom in July.

In this way many treasures may be grown but it is where a piece of wild wood exists that the wild gardener who is also a plantsman will find the greatest delight. In such a place he may grow the meconopses, the fabulous blue poppy *Meconopsis betonicifolia* and the larger *grandis*—the hybrid *sheldonii*—too if he can get it and the yellow *regia* and *integrifolia* with their exquisitely silky-furred winter rosettes. Of these *regia* is definitely monocarpic and one grows it principally for the beauty of its winter rosettes and after flowering it dies. A proportion of *betonicifolia* flower for several seasons before dying, and some are truly perennial as are a higher proportion of *grandis*, while × *sheldonii* is the most reliable with the best and bluest flowers of all. On acid soil all are magnificent and well worth the trouble which the dedicated woodland gardener will take to raise a batch or two each year from seed.

Another woodland speciality is the giant lily—*Cardio-crinum giganteum*—the flowers of which, carried on six- to ten-foot stems, need maximum wind-shelter. Most distinctive in appearance with shining heart-shaped foliage and long narrow trumpet flowers borne in elongated racemes of twelve or more. The flowers are a gleaming white, purple-stained within and sweetly scented. The cardiocrinum needs deep rich soil and the bulb takes several years to flower (usually five) after which it dies, leaving behind offsets, each of which should be separately planted in specially prepared sites. Some growers dig several pits, three feet deep, into which they throw their garden refuse, building up a compost-heap *in situ* for a year or so before they plant the bulbs. Two-year-old bulbs make the best initial purchase and one might buy a few each year until one's original cardiocrinums flower and yield their own offsets. In this way an increasing stock and continuity of flowering will be assured after the first bulbs flower.

A true lily which is especially suited to woodland cultivation is *Lilium canadense* which carries four-foot stems with terminal clusters of drooping trumpet flowers, orange in colour and freely spotted with brown. It needs a cool, moist, partly shaded position and deep leaf-soil. The golden *hansonii* and the orange-scarlet turkscap lily *pardalinum* enjoy similar conditions, as do the martagons, the Backhouse hybrids and the glamorous *auratum*.

More prosaic but none the less appealing in its own quiet way is *Mertensia virginica*, the Virginian Cowslip. Easy enough in its homeland where it carpets the woodland much as do the British bluebells over here, it is often not quick to make progress in this country. This is because its need for moisture and shelter are not fully realized. In moist, sandy peat in a sheltered nook it will make itself at home and show the full beauty of its drooping clusters of violet-blue flowers carried on eighteen-inch stems and the attractions of its large blue-grey leaves. It is worth the trouble necessary to ensure success but it is essentially a subject for the plant-lover's garden rather than for the very busy person to whom the attraction of a wild garden is that it can in part take care of itself.

One of the most delightful shrubby treasures is the low-growing creeping *Philesia magellanica* with its small dark linear leaves and its lovely rose-red waxy bells that droop like those of a lapageria. It enjoys just the same type of soil and situation as does the mertensia. Some of the finest rhododendrons, too, are gems for sheltered acid-soil sites. Among the best of these are such large-leafed giants as *sino-grande* with its shiny, leathery 'elephant's ears', *ficto lacteum* with its rusty orange felt and the tree-like *falconeri* which may need twenty years to bear its magnificent yellow trusses. Some of the more tender scented species will be hardy on a woodland slope where the frost can drain away and where the branches of deciduous tree offer a protective canopy. One of the most reliable of these is the white form of *bullatum* with its embossed leaves and fragrant white trumpets. In such a position one can experiment also with the early-flowering species and hybrids that yield their blossoms from November to March, affording opulent flowers for cutting and helping to chase away winter's gloom.

One of the most satisfactory of the winter-blooming rhododendrons is *mucronulatum* which was recently award-ed the First Class Certificate of the Royal Horticultural Society for its excellence in flower. Rosy-purple in colour its butterfly-blossoms resemble those of some members of the azalea series and as with those of its azalea-relations are borne on the bare branches. In mild areas the first blooms open in January. In fact, with us in North Wales, *Rhododendron mucronulatum* is often in flower in December. The delicate-looking blooms, however, will withstand a frost that temporarily flattens the hellebores. Really severe frost, of course, turns the blossoms to pulp but one of the chief merits of this species—and one which sets it above the closely related *dauricum*—is the fact that it does not open all its flowers at once, so usually there is a second, and even a third, crop to replace those damaged by the weather. Lightly built, this rhododendron forms a twiggy bush that may eventually reach five feet in height and as much in width. It makes a good companion for the spidery-gold witch-hazels and as its buds and flowers open and last well indoors any restrictive pruning should be carried out while it is in flower so that one can enjoy the surplus growths indoors.

*R.* 'Nobleanum' is quite different in character. It is a hybrid and resembles the well-known hardy hybrids in growth and leaf and in the shape of its rosy-crimson flower trusses. The type usually opens in February in North Wales but there is a lovely warm pink variety known as *R.* 'Nobleanum Venustum' which opens its first buds in November and flowers during mild spells until March. There is also a white variety which is the last of the three to bloom. In cold districts and in bad winters the flowering of this hybrid is retarded until spring and so is worth planting in all but the bleakest districts.

Nearer *mucronulatum* in type, but evergreen, *R. moupinense* is a beautiful species. Its flowers are of the azalea-type and either milky-white or a softly pretty pink freckled with tan. For many years this rhododendron remains dwarf enough for the protection of a polythene cloche or bag—a boon if a sudden frost threatens its opened flowers.

True winter-blooming plants, these rhododendrons will be followed in February or March by the well-known lilac-mauve 'Praecox', the rosy 'Tessa' and the graceful *lutescens* whose primrose-yellow blossoms give a happy foretaste of spring.

At about the same time blooms the larger *fargesii* with scented lilac blooms and the closely related *oreodoxa* which together will give a month of bloom.

Another scented rhododendron which is best in woodland is the May-flowering 'Loderi' with huge but shapely flower trusses and a cool cucumber-like scent.

Species azaleas such as *vaseyi* in pale pink, the vivid rose *albrechtii* and the rich magenta *reticulatum* may also be grown. They are very hardy, however, and do not really need such shelter although *reticulatum* does need a rather moist very acid soil to do well. On the other hand the shell-pink *schlippenbachii* with its large shell-pink flowers needs to be protected from the wind. A camellia that deserves woodland conditions is the fragrant *C. sasanqua* 'Narumi-gata' (*oleifera*) with wide-petalled, appleblossom flowers in December.

Several lovely primula species which are less easy-going than their fellows can be recommended only for the plantsman who is able to give them exactly the conditions they need. One of these is *Primula vialii* with flowers close-packed into a spike of scarlet and lavender looking for all the world like tiny red-hot pokers.

With its emerald leaves and ice-white flowers dusted with golden meal, the snow-primula, *P. chionantha*, makes a lovely contrast with *P. vialii* and with the coloured candelabras. The easiest to satisfy of the difficult Nivalis section, it will do well at the bottom of a shady bank with its toes in the ditch, in moist rhododendron woodland or in a heavy loam. When happy it will seed itself but it is as well to be on the safe side and collect some seed each year. As with all primulas and gentians I like to sow the seed in January (in a compost of sand and peat) to top the pans with chippings to prevent the soil caking and to stand them on the north side of a hedge or building to weather, taking them into the warmth in March to speed up germination.

Easier than the two species just discussed *P. sieboldii* is an effective plant that is not these days often seen. With large flowers, reminiscent of greenhouse primulas, on tall stalks and with crinkly fresh green leaves it is worth growing in quantity. There are several named varieties in lavender, rose and white and Messrs. Thompson and Morgan of Ipswich can usually offer seed which should give rise to a good mixed colour range.

Double flowers in general are to be avoided in the wild garden but I would always make an exception to grow the old double lilac and double white primroses in a shady cool spot where I could watch over them, dividing them when the clumps became too big and pulling out encroaching grass and weeds. Some find them hard to grow and in my time I have lost several but always the lilac and the double white have proved easy and willing. Of the two the lilac is the most generally acknowledged to be reliable. I find it enjoys a rather moist soil and not having supplies of cow-manure (as advocated by the pundits) I feed my plants in spring, just before flowering, with a little general flower fertilizer pricked lightly in.

# PART TWO

*A Wild Gardener's
Plant Dictionary*

## SECTION I

# Corms, Bulbs, Tubers, etc., for the Wild Garden and Naturalization

꙳꙳꙳꙳꙳

**AGAPANTHUS**
*Moist, well-drained soil*
*Sun*

This blue African Lily has proved much hardier than was formerly believed. The species *umbellatus* (*mooreanus*) with flower stems a foot to eighteen-inches in height and the deep blue 'Headbourne Hybrids' evolved by the Hon. Lewis Palmer and now in commerce are reliably hardy in moist but well-drained loam in all but the frostiest gardens. They are delightful planted near a woodland stream (but above water level) or to form a cool band of blue, continuing the effect of the earlier *Iris sibirica* where no water exists. Heedless of chalk they will grow on downland or heathland alike.

**ALLIUM**
*Most like full sun*

Most flowering garlics appreciate a dryish soil in full sun. An exception to this rule is the Chinese *beesianum* with its drooping heads of blue bells on foot-high stems. It prefers a cool moist position.

Other recommended species are the tall ($2\frac{1}{2}$ to 3 ft) *aflatunense* with spherical heads of lilac-purple, *albo-pilosum* with lilac-pink heads on two-foot stems, the five-foot *giganteum* with violet globular heads, the gay little golden *moly* which with its looser umbels will grow anywhere, *rosenbachianum* with purple-blue spheres and the magenta *sphaerocephalum*.

ALSTROEMERIA
*Well-drained site*
*Sun*

The common *aurantiaca* is easy enough for the wild garden and will make a mass of brilliant orange in a sunny spot. The roots should be planted six inches deep as soon as they are received in spring. The variety *A. aurantiaca lutea* is equally easy and just as showy. Both are hardy in a well-drained site in full sun.

ANEMONE
*Requirements vary*
*according to*
*species*

From the Italian woods, the glorious blue, daisy-flowered *apennina* is one of the loveliest of all anemones. It blooms in late spring and is fine for the woodland garden and will spread readily to form delightful sheets and pools of soft sky-blue. Best moved when its ferny foliage is still green, just after the flowers are over, it is sometimes difficult to start from dry tubers. This difficulty can be overcome by soaking the tubers in water for forty-eight hours before planting. There is a white form which makes a pleasant contrast to the blue. The rather similar but earlier flowering *Anemone blanda* from Greece needs sun to open its very early flowers. In a warm place it will often begin to bloom at the end of February. Pink and white varieties are available as well as the blue. All are pretty and planted two to three inches deep in well-drained soil will usually seed freely.

The English equivalent is *A. nemorosa*, the wild wood anemone. Charming though the common white type may be there are several finer forms which may be added near to a path or stream or in the more frequented places. *A.n.* 'Robinsoniana', 'Allenii' and 'Royal Blue' vary in shade from golden wreathed grey-blue to almost sky. There is also a fine frilly double white, a petaloid-centred white with flowers like small frilly pincushions and a very large single white.

ANTHERICUM
*Dappled shade*

*Paradisea (Anthericum) liliastrum*, St. Bruno's Lily, is a bulb for orchard or meadow grass. Its slender snowy trumpets are carried two feet high above grassy foliage in June and July. To avoid damage when the grass is cut it should be planted near the boles of the trees, the dappled shade of which it enjoys.

ARISAEMA
*Woodland*

'Jack-in-the-Pulpit', *A. triphyllum* is a characterful plant of the woodlands of the eastern United States. Like a hooded arum with bright green spathes and pitcher-flowers striped in brown and purple followed by scarlet berries it grows easily in a moist leafy spot.

ARISARUM
*Woodland or*
*Hedgerow*

The Mouse Plant, *A. proboscideum*, is useful as ground cover in a minor way while in June appear the mouse-like arum pitchers. They have long tails which disappear in a quaint way into the masses of small fresh-green, arrow-shaped leaves. Very easy, it thrives anywhere that is not too dry and is particularly good in woodland.

ARUM
*Wood or*
*Hedgerow*

*A. italicum pictum* and *A.i. marmoratum* enjoy similar conditions to the arisarum. With their prettily marked leaves they are valuable to give winter colour.

CAMASSIA
*Any reasonable*
*soil*
*Sun or shade*

These North American bulbs are easy to grow. They will do well in sun or shade in grass, heath or woodland and with their tall stems of starry flowers they are effective to give summer colour. *C. cusickii* pale blue, the deeper blue or white *leichtlinii* and *quamash (esculenta)* all seed freely.

CHIONODOXA
*Sun*

The little Glories of the Snow with their sky-blue and white, rose or gentian-blue flowers are among the prettiest of early bulbs. They will naturalize freely in stony places and are ideal for a quarry or a cliff where they will interbreed also with the scillas if any are present. They will grow, too, in open ground in woodland but they do not do very well in grass where their place should be taken by the stronger growing *Muscari* 'Heavenly Blue'. *C. gigantea* is the tallest growing species and carries white-centred violet-blue flowers. *C. luciliae* is one of the prettiest with sky-blue, white-centred stars. *C. sardensis* is the deep gentian-blue species. White and pink forms exist of *gigantea* and *luciliae* but they are not as attractive in the wild as are the blues.

COLCHICUM
*Grass or among shrubs*

Sometimes wrongly known as 'Autumn Crocus', the colchicums in autumn carry substantial chalices of rose-purple, lavender or white. They grow well in orchard grass, woodland, heathland or downland where they are best planted in the shelter of shrubs or boulders for protection from the autumn gales. *C. agrippinum* is the best of the chequered forms available; the soft mauve *autumnale* and its white form *a. album* are the slender, long-stemmed colchicums seen in the Alps and some parts of Britain where they have naturalized. There is also a double form of this species. *Byzantinum* is rosy-lilac, sturdy and free-flowering; the rosy *speciosum*, its varieties *album* and *bornmuelleri* (rosy-lilac with a white centre) are the sturdiest and best of the species—Farrer rightly said of *speciosum*: it is 'One of the most noble and beautiful plants in the world'. There are also numerous hybrids mostly good and also vigorous.

CONVALLARIA
*Wood. Weed suppressor*

*C. majalis*, the Lily of the Valley with its pristine, scented bells and cool foliage is one of the best subjects for naturalizing in woodland. Liking shady places, leaf-mouldy soil and humus

13 *Cornus canadensis*—a reliable and picturesque ground cover for acid soil.

14 *Galax aphylla* with its polished leaves and white flower-spikes is a classic subject for acid soil. Its foliage is evergreen and assumes scarlet tints in the winter months.

it may also be made at home in prepared, fairly rich soil under a hedgebank or in the less-wet part of a ditch garden. Its roots mat closely, keeping out all weeds. There is a double form and also a rare rose-pink variety. Some poor pink forms are sometimes sold. So unless one can be sure of obtaining the true *C. majalis* 'Rosea' it is as well to keep to the ordinary delightful white.

CORYDALIS
*Easy anywhere*
*Spreads and seeds*

The little golden fumitory, *C. lutea*, with its ferny foliage is a plant that everybody knows spreads rapidly in poor, stony places in sun or even in rooty woodland soil and is useful to add colour to a quarry garden, cliff, old wall or Cornish hedge. There is a rather rare white-flowered form which is also pretty. *C. solida* has pinky-purple flower sprays above grey ferny foliage and is equally easy. If anywhere it does best in woodland where it will make a light and pretty ground cover.

CROCUS
*Sun. Good*
  *drainage*

Two autumn-flowering species will naturalize readily, seeding themselves about in sunny, stony places. They are *C. speciosus* and *C. kotschyanus* (*zonatus*). Both are pretty but the cups of *kotschyanus* are pale lilac whereas those of *speciosus* are a good deep blue. Given sharp drainage in full sun both will seed rapidly. *Speciosus* will also succeed in light woodland.

Best known of the winter/early-spring crocus species is undoubtedly *C. tomasinianus* which will seed itself about and increase rapidly, flowering in three years from seed. It has been said that mice will not touch the corms of this species but in my garden they seem to eat them as readily as those of any other crocus. Crushed mothballs set with each group at planting time are an effective deterrent. *C. chrysanthus*,

I

*susianus, aureus, vernus* and *versicolor* are also satisfactory. Of these the best colonizers are perhaps *aureus* and *vernus*. With its golden chalices, *aureus* makes a particularly effective companion for the lavender *tomasinianus*.

The large Dutch hybrids are effective in grass where they will increase vegetatively. A mixture of blue, purple, white and striped varieties gives the best effect.

CYCLAMEN
*Half-shade. Good
drainage*

The autumn-flowering *C. neapolitanum* is the most generally used species for wild-garden planting. It is happy under shrubs or at the base of large deciduous trees. Sometimes, where drainage is too sharp and tree roots too hungry, it flags in the hot September sun, so half-shade and a leaf-mouldy site should be offered. White and pink forms are available and all have the ivy-leaves of the species with their beautiful filigree pattern of pale, frosty jade. *Repandum* also is hardy and easy. It will often seed in grass. Flowering in spring its sharp-petalled crimson flowers are lovely in short orchard grass or under trees or shrubs. It will grow also in a vertical crevice of a wall as in its native Italy or on a hedgebank. It, too, has attractive leaves. *Europaeum* flowers in July and is a success in some parts of the country but not in North Wales. With us the leaves linger for a season or two but it seldom flowers. This is disappointing as all the other species do so well. *Orbiculatum* and its variety *coum* flower in the winter and are treasures for those parts of the wild garden which can be kept under observation. They are not difficult to grow but they are relatively expensive and need to be planted where they can be enjoyed.

Cyclamen are sometimes slow to establish from dried corms. I always plant these first in moist peat in a warm place and wait until the leaves start to appear before planting them out. They may be purchased also as growing plants in pots and set out with scarcely a check. Seed may be bought and all the species mentioned may be readily raised therefrom.

Sometimes it is difficult to see which way up the corms should be planted. *Neapolitanum* roots from the top; *orbiculatum* and some other species from the base. Usually dried whiskers of roots remain as an indication. When in doubt it is quite safe to plant the corms on their sides and allow nature to adjust matter for herself.

ENDYMION
(SCILLA)
*Woodland or Grass*
*Part shade or sun*

Formerly known as species of the genus Scilla and now classified as *Endymion*, the bluebells are all good wild garden subjects. The native bluebell (*Scilla non-scripta*) and the garden forms (*S. hispanica*) have pink and white varieties as well as the blue. All are worth growing and will seed themselves readily.

ERANTHIS
*Grass or at the*
*front of shrubs*

*E. hyemalis* is the earliest and cheapest. Where it is well suited it will spread happily. If it dislikes one's soil and situation nothing will make it grow but where it fails the larger hybrid *E.* × *tubergeniana* will often succeed and is worth planting in one or two special groups for the joyful picture of its large golden cups gleaming above their dark green ruffs. Not usually setting seed, *E.* × *tubergeniana* will increase slowly but surely by vegetative means.

ERYTHRONIUM
*Woodland*

The European *dens-canis* is the cheapest of the Dog's Tooth Violets to plant in quantity. It should not be planted in too much shade as the sun is needed fully to open the pretty reflexed flowers. The North American species are taller and even more beautiful. They flower a little later. Expensive to obtain they seed readily in moist woodland soil. *E.* 'White Beauty', *californicum* and the golden *tuolumnense* and its hybrids may usually be bought. 'Pink Beauty' and the pink *revolutum* are very difficult to get but they can be raised from seed sown in a shady, moist place. Unfortunately they take five years to flower but each season their spotted, trout-marked leaves increase in size and beauty. Seed of the large flowered lavender *hendersonii* also may sometimes be obtained.

**FRITILLARIA**
*Grass or*
*Woodland*

Best for the wild garden is the native *F. meleagris* which flowers in April with its drooping bells, chequered in purple and mauve or unmarked in white. Its position should be on the moist side rather than the dry, otherwise it is easy to satisfy and will usually seed itself and naturalize. The tall, stately *imperialis*, the Crown Imperial, makes a handsome group in woodland and may be obtained in orange and yellow forms. The large bulbs are hollow in the middle so to avoid any possibility of their rotting from accumulated moisture in the crown they should be planted on their sides.

**GALANTHUS**
*Choose species to*
*suit position*

The common *G. nivalis* has naturalized in many woodlands and churchyards and is the easiest and cheapest species to use in woodland. It will often do well in short grass, particularly in moist places, and is at home on hedgebanks and under orchard trees. The other species cheap enough to plant in quantity is *elwesii* which prefers a sunny, well-drained site. There are many other species and varieties most of which will naturalize where they are well suited. To those who would know more about them I can recommend the Royal Horticultural

Society's publication *Snowdrops and Snowflakes* written by Sir Frederick Stern who is an authority on the genus.

**GALTONIA**
*Grass or among shrubs*

Of this genus *candicans* is the species most likely to prove useful to the wild gardener. Handsome spires of solid ivory bells are carried on four-foot stems in late July and August. It will do well in any good soil.

**GLADIOLUS**
*Sun and good drainage*

The magenta *byzantinus* is the easiest of the wild gladioli—others that will succeed with in a sunny place are *segetum, communis* and *tristis*. The latter is the most tender and should only be tried in really warm gardens.

**HEPATICA**
*Woodsy soil*

The members of this genus though delightful are pets for special places rather than rampageous plants for the rough and tumble of wild garden life. The white form of *triloba* and the blue and lilac forms of *transsilvanica* (*angulosa*) are the most robust and will establish happily in a moist, woodsy place or on a hedgebank or among ferns on a mossy wall. I have seen it stated that they do best on limy soils but this has not been my experience. I have grown hepaticas for many years and I find they are indifferent as to whether soil is alkaline or otherwise.

**HERMODACTYLUS**
**TUBEROSUS**
*Any soil in sun or shade*

The little velvety green and purple-black Snake's Head Iris flowers in March and April and is an attractive wild garden plant that succeeds in any reasonable soil.

**LEUCOJUM**
*Variable*

Two species, *L. vernum* that bears its sturdy green-tipped white bells on four-to six-inch stems at snowdrop time and the taller *L. aestivum* with its three or four drooping snowflake flowers in May are useful in the wild garden. *L. vernum* will grow in sun or shade but *aestivum* does best in a damp soil and excels by the streamside or pool.

**LILIUM**
*Varied*

From the old-fashioned yellow or mallow purple turkscaps of *pyrenaicum*, which flowers in May with a somewhat overpowering scent, to the massive and glamorous trumpets of *auratum* there is a variety of lilies to challenge the wild gardener.

Some are easy such as *pyrenaicum*, the white and purple varieties of the turkscap *martagon* and the newer hybrids 'Destiny' and 'Enchantment' with their bold upturned chalices in yellow and nasturtium orange. Others must have conditions exactly to their liking or they will not succeed. The tall brown-spotted orange turkscap *henryi* is willing enough in a vegetable soil that is not too acid. The golden throated *auratum* on the other hand will not establish itself on limy ground. *Canadense* with its pendent orange bells comes from the Canadian prairies and will grow in orchard grass. It needs an airy, open site. *Hansonii*, with its reflexed petals of thick gold will usually do well in woodland. Leaf mould and a shady site are what it needs. The Panther Lily, *pardalinum*, needs moist soil. Both *L. monadelphum* and *szovitsianum* are easy and lovely with cool yellow trumpets but their price puts them beyond the reach of most of us. For vigorous, easy, reasonably-priced lilies that can be relied on to thrive and to increase, one cannot do better than the 'Fiesta' hybrids, the 'Mid-Century' group (to which 'Destiny' and 'Enchantment' belong) and the 'Bellingham' strain.

Also, where no other lilies are grown, the Tiger lilies, *tigrinum* in its various forms are easy, cheap and vigorous. They do, however, harbour a virus which may be passed on to other lily species.

**MUSCARI**
*Easy anywhere*

For the wild garden, whether grass or woodland, *M. armenaicum* 'Heavenly Blue' is the most satisfactory. Vigorous and robust it will seed itself about and spread freely. For special places the light blue *M.a.* 'Cantab' and the white *M. botryoides album* may be introduced to give variety.

**NARCISSUS**
*Grass or among shrubs*

Of the larger varieties the following have been found among the most reliable to naturalize in grass: 'Magnificence', 'Flower Carpet', 'Carlton', 'John Evelyn' (apricot cup), 'Mount Hood' (white trumpet), 'Dick Wellband' (red cup), 'Mrs. R. O. Backhouse' (pink trumpet), 'Semper Avanti' (orange crown), 'Van Sion' (old double daffodil). To these may be added the old 'Pheasant's Eye' narcissus which is at its best in grass and such smaller varieties as the lovely pale little 'W. P. Milner', the miniature golden-trumpeted Tenby daffodil *N. obvallaris*, the paler Lent Lily *N. pseudo-narcissus* and the *cyclamineus* hybrids 'March Sunshine', 'February Gold' and 'Peeping Tom'. In damp, woodsy places or in moist grass the tiny, shy-eared *cyclamineus* will succeed while the Hoop Petticoat daffodil *bulbocodium conspicuus* enjoys a similar but slightly drier spot.

**ORNITHOGALUM**
*Easy anywhere*

The 'Star of Bethlehem', *O. umbellatum* and the earlier-flowering *nutans* are easy and attractive with their silvery, green-striped flowers. Ready colonizers and inexpensive to buy they are among a wild gardener's best friends.

**OXALIS**
*Varied*

*O. rosea* (floribunda) of cottage gardens and its white variety (*f. alba*) are colourful and easy for quarry, cliff or wall. The wild wood sorrel is pretty in woodland and to be encouraged.

RANUNCULUS
*Moist soil*

*R. ficaria*, the Celandine is always attractive and its large *major* form is to be sought after and treasured as are also the white and copper varieties and the double.

SANGUINARIA
*Woodland*

The Canadian Blood-Root with its lovely grey-green palmate leaves and white anemone-flowers is also a treasure as is its double variety *S. canadensis* 'Flore Pleno'. Both need shade and leaf-mould. They should be planted in a special site where they can be admired and cherished.

SCHIZOSTYLIS
*Moist, well-drained soil—sun or shade*

In their native South Africa the schizostylis flower at the end of the rainy season, therefore they need more moisture than many gardeners realize. I have never known them do better than when grown in good humusy loam which retains the moisture in summer but is well drained and so does not lie cold and stagnant in winter. In the western half of Britain, at any rate, they are easy and spread rapidly. They do well around orchard trees or at the forefront of shrubs. The type is a good red, *S. coccinea*, but 'Mrs. Heggarty' (shrimp-pink) and the satin pink 'Viscountess Byng' are also good. The latter flowers late and is a valuable November/ December plant in mild districts.

SCILLA
*Sun*

These lovely little blue-flowered bulbs are generous and easy—as well as seeding themselves they hybridize with the chionodoxas and give rise to some very pretty forms. *Bifolia* is one of the earliest with deep gentian-blue open bells on slender spikes in early March. *Sibirica* also is showy and cheap enough to plant freely.

TRILLIUM
*Woodland*

Liking leaf-mould and semi-shade the trilliums, the North American Wake Robin or Trinity Flower are ideal plants for the wild wood. Several species are available but none are more, pleasing than *T. grandiflorum* with its snowy three-petalled flowers.

TRITELEIA
(MILLA)
correctly Ipheion
*Sun and good
drainage*

Although the botanists have changed the name of this pretty flower it is usually listed as *Triteleia uniflorum*. With grassy leaves and milky-blue starry flowers it is delightful and easy in a sunny, stony spot.

TULIPA
*Sun*

One may naturalize the Darwin tulips in grass otherwise only the three species, the scarlet *sprengeri* which spreads by seed, the yellow *sylvestris* and the pink *saxatilis* which increase stoloniferously can be considered as wild garden subjects. The last is suitable only for a hot rocky ledge or stony, sunny bank.

SECTION II

## Perennials and Biennials
## Herbaceous Subjects and Ground Cover
## for the Wild Garden

ACANTHUS
4 ft × 2 ft
*Ground cover*

The handsome *A. mollis* is a useful wild garden plant for heavy soil and full sun. With sculptured shiny leaves and tall spikes of pink, purple-flushed flowers it is a most attractive plant and one which forms vigorous clumps to keep down weeds.

AJUGA
½ ft × 1–3 ft
(spreading)
*Ground cover*

Best in slightly moist soil in sun or half-shade, the creeping bugles make excellent dense ground cover. *A. reptans* 'Atropurpurea' (purple leaves) and the variegated 'Multicoloralis' (Rainbow') and 'Metallica' are all good. *A. genevensis* makes large clumps of deep green leaves and has bright blue flower spikes. However it does not spread so rapidly by runners as do the others—a 'bear' point in the wild garden whereas it might be a 'bull' point for the conventional border.

ANAPHALIS
½ ft × 2 ft
*Sun*

Grey foliaged plants for cliff or quarry with fluffy white 'everlasting' flowers.

ANCHUSA
3–5 ft × 2 ft
(flopping)
*Any soil. Sun*

*A. italica* is a plant for an orchard garden or for any rough places. Though short-lived in some places it usually seeds and can be readily propagated from root cuttings. Indeed any pieces of broken-off root can usually be relied upon to grow. The tall 'Opal' and 'Morning Glory' flop about if not staked. In the wild garden, of course, stakes are out of the question and flopping is not a bad fault enabling, as it does, the plant to act as ground cover. 'Loddon Royalist' and 'Royal Blue' are shorter, sturdier and more upright varieties.

**ALCHEMILLA**
1½ ft × 1 ft
(increasing in spread)
*Ground cover*

The Lady's Mantle, *A. mollis*, has attractive downy rounded leaves and is dense enough in growth to keep down weeds. Tiny greeny-yellow starry flowers are borne in airy sprays in late May and early June.

**ANEMONE**
2–5 ft × 1½–2 ft
*Ground cover*

The Japanese anemones are vigorous, spreading plants for woodland, waterside or orchard garden. *A. hupehensis* has many varieties in white or pink. Most are good. They flower in September whereas *A. vitifolia* flowers in August. It too has both pink and white forms and is even more vigorous, forming close thickets of stems and colonizing freely.

**ANTHEMIS**
1 ft × 2 ft
*Ground cover for sun*

*A. cupaniana* is a fine weed suppressor for stony, sunny places. Evergreen or rather ever-grey with feathery foliage and shimmering display of pure white daisies in June it is a good plant for cliff or quarry gardens where it will drape over the rocks in silvery cushions.

**AQUILEGIA**
2 ft × 1 ft

Pretty almost anywhere, colonizing by seed and very hardy, good strains of columbine will enhance any wild garden. *A. alpina*, 'Munstead White' (*vulgaris nivea*), 'Mrs. Scott Elliott's', 'Crimson Star' and *longissima* hybrids are all good strains with which to start.

**ARTEMISIA**

Useful plants for sunny places in poor soil. *A.*

1½–4 ft × 2 ft
*Ground cover.*
   *Mainly for sun*

*abrotanum* ('Southernwood' or 'Old Man') *ludoviciana, canescens* and *pontica* are hardy in well-drained places. The more tender *arborescens* is safe on a cliff or quarry face. *A. lactiflora* with its cream astilbe-like plumes is a plant for moister places and will stand shade.

ARUNCUS
4 ft × 2 ft

The Goat's Beard, *A. sylvester*, can be an outrageous weed, seeding dangerously. To avoid this it is wisest to grow only the male form. One can then enjoy its broad ferny foliage and creamy plumes without fear of the consequences. It will grow in any reasonably moist soil in sun or shade.

ASPHODELINE
3 ft × 1 ft

*A. lutea*, the yellow asphodel, is a handsome plant with a cluster of glaucous basal leaves from which arise the stately flower spikes of silky yellow. It does well in sun in any good soil.

ASTILBE
2–3 ft × 2 ft
*Ground cover for*
   *damp places*

With their close mats of roots the astilbes are efficient weed-suppressors in any moist or even wet soil. Good varieties are: 'Fanal' and 'Granat' (crimson), 'King Albert' (white), 'Amethyst', 'Irrlicht' (white), 'Salmon Queen', 'Gloria' (pink) and 'Cattleya' (lilac-pink).

BERGENIA
1 ft × 1 ft
(spreading rapidly)
*Ground cover*

Although rather formal to my eye for the wild garden, the bergenias are excellent ground cover, their large, paddle-shaped leaves suppressing all other growth and their fat spikes of flower in early spring are always welcome. The leaves of some species colour well in winter particularly if they are growing in sunny, well drained places. Best for this effect are *cordifolia purpurea* and *crassifolia*. There is also the more expensive 'Ballawley Hybrid' (Delbees) with leaves which become dark crimson-purple in the cold weather. This cultivar, however, needs an especially sheltered place and part shade, so for the wild garden generally the two species mentioned are best.

**BORAGO**
(prostrate, spreading)
*Weed suppressor.*
*Any soil. Sun*
*or shade*

*B. laxiflora* is a pretty plant with its airy sprays of tiny pointed bells in turquoise-blue. Its leaves are rough, hairy, and it sends out leafy stolons which root to form new plants. It also seeds itself freely and can be relied to cover a good area with dense, weed-suppressing growth. It is attractive used with the copper-leafed bugle *Ajuga reptans* 'Atropurpurea', the burnished leaves of which make a lovely foil for the dainty flowers of this borage.

**BRUNNERA**
$1\frac{1}{2}$ ft × 2 ft
*Ground cover*

*B. macrophylla* (*Anchusa myosotidiflora*) has large heart-shaped leaves which are valuable for weed suppression. To these are added vivid sprays of bright blue forget-me-not-like flowers in spring. Does best in soil that is not too dry in half-shade—a woodland or orchard plant.

**CALTHA**
1 ft × 1 ft
*Moist soil*

The Kingcups are pretty spring-flowering plants for moist soil or the waterside. There is a double variety which I dislike although I know many people find it showy, an extra fine and vigorous cultivar known as 'Tyerman's Variety' and a white form *C. palustris alba*.

**CAMPANULA**
Varying heights
*Sun or shade*

*C. portenschlagiana* (*muralis*) and *poscharskyana* are two vigorous trailing species for a quarry or wall. The lovely pale grey-lilac × *burghaltii* grows erectly to two feet and is pretty anywhere. The cluster-flowered, purple *glomerata* is a runner for sun. *Lactiflora* is best for woodland or a sheltered orchard as it is so tall (6 ft) as to be blown down in windy places. *Persicifolia* is shorter (3 ft) and in both its white and blue forms seeds freely. Closely planted it makes good, dense ground cover.

**CENTAUREA**
1½ ft × 2 ft
*Sun*

*C. dealbata*, the old-fashioned cornflower, is pretty anywhere in orchard or grass. Long-lived it forms big clumps and sows itself about.

**CENTRANTHUS**
1½ ft × 2 ft
*Sun. Poor soil*

The 'Valerian' in white and shades of pink and red is a lovely, easy plant to naturalize in quarries, on cliffs or walls. Flowering from May to August it is one of the glories of summer in such places and its dense mats of blue-green leaves are cheerful and attractive all the year. It seeds widely usually sowing itself in the most appropriate places.

**CIMICIFUGA**
5 ft × 2 ft
*Moist soil. Shade*

An attractive woodland plant with ferny leaves and plumes of white flowers. It spreads slowly and closely planted makes useful ground cover.

**CORNUS**
½ ft × 1 ft
(spreading)
*Woodland or heath*

With its pretty four-petalled white flowers and handsome rosettes of leaves *Cornus canadensis* is a pleasing ground-covering plant for sun or shade in woodsy or peaty, sandy soil. It will not thrive where lime is present.

**CROCOSMIA**
2 ft (spreading)
*Any soil. Sun or shade*

This is the Montbretia with sword-like leaves and sprays of orange-red flowers. It is a useful plant to naturalize and is particularly happy and effective by the waterside.

**CURTONUS**
(Antholyza)
4 ft (spreading)
*Sun. Good soil*

Virtually a giant Montbretia with larger, more handsome leaves and sprays of orange-red flower.

**CYNOGLOSSUM**
1½ ft × 2 ft
*Ground cover. Any soil. Sun*

*C. nervosum* (Hound's Tongue) with its gentian-blue flowers and rough green leaves is a useful wild garden plant. There is also a biennial species *C. amabile* which once planted will seed itself freely and naturalize much as will the common forget-me-not to which, flowering later, it makes a useful successor.

**DIANTHUS**
1 ft × 2 ft
*Ground cover. Sun.*
*Well-drained*
*soil*

*D. gratianopolitanus* (*D. caesius*) the Cheddar Pink, various alpine varieties and the Highland Hybrids will seed themselves about and naturalize. They are attractive and in keeping on a cliff, in a quarry or on walls.

**DICENTRA**
1½ ft × 1 ft
*Cool soil. Shade*
*or sun*

The pink *D. formosa* and its white variety *alba* with their fresh green fernery are pretty wild garden plants for moist soil.

**DIGITALIS**
5 ft × 1 ft
*Naturalized. Any*
*soil*

All the foxgloves are useful colonizers for the wild garden. The 'Shirley' strain, 'Sutton's White', 'Sutton's Apricot' and 'Sutton's Yellow' are all worth raising from seed and planting freely. Thereafter they will seed themselves. Of the perennial species the yellow *D. grandiflora* (*ambigua*) (2 ft) and mauve-buff × *mertonensis* are good.

**DORONICUM**
2 ft × 2 ft
*Any soil. Shade*

Showy in the early Spring with their bright yellow daisies the doronicums are trouble-free. The well-known *D. orientale* 'Miss Mason' is one of the earliest, starting to bloom in April, and can be followed by *D. pardalianches* 'Golden Bunch' which flowers from May to the end of June. *D. plantagineum excelsum* ('Harpur Crewe') needs moister soil than the others. All will grow in grass.

**EPIMEDIUM**
½ ft (spreading)
*Ground cover. Not*
*too dry a position*

The epimediums are handsome ground cover plants for sun or shade and will succeed wherever the soil does not dry out. With their good leaves and airy flower sprays they are always attractive and most species colour well in autumn and winter. *E. grandiflorum, perralderianum, pinnatum,* × *warleyense, and* × *versicolor* are all good 'doers'

ERYNGIUM
1–2 ft × 2 ft
*Most enjoy well-
drained soil. Sun*

Our native Sea Holly, *E. maritimum* is a useful soil-retainer and is pleasant with its spiny leaves and misty amethyst flowers. *Tripartitum* is a good one, freely branching and carrying many blue 'thistle'-like flowers. *Giganteum* is a biennial but seeds itself. It is attractive with prickly white collars to the blue flower-heads. *Oliverianum, planum* and *amethystinum* are other good species.

EUPHORBIA
Size varies accord-
   ing to species
*Sun any soil.
   Ground cover*

Handsome and unusual, the Spurges are inter-esting wild garden plants. Some such as *E. veneta (wulfenii)* are so large that they keep down weeds for an area of three or four square feet. Statuesque at any time of the year the greeny yellow flower buds in spring heighten the attraction of the plant as do the strange love-bird green flowers. *E. sikkimensis* is another large-growing species as is the newer *griffithii* which is very handsome in early summer with its bright orange flower-heads. *E. epithymoides*, on the other hand, is a lowly carpeter but not less cheerful and attractive than the other species. All are easily raised from seed.

FILIPENDULA
3–4 ft × 1½ ft
*Moist soil*

*F. purpurea (Spiraea palmata)* is a handsome plant for the waterside or for wet ground. It forms big clumps from which arise large leaves crowned by flat feathery heads of cherry-crim-son.

   *F. ulmaria* 'Plena' is the double Meadow Sweet with sweet scent and creamy white heads of flowers. The ordinary form of the Meadow Sweet may also be used but seeding rather freely as it does can become too invasive even for the wild garden.

FOENICULUM
4–6 ft × 3 ft
*Sun and poor soil*

The Fennel is a beautiful plant for late summer effect in dry places and will grow even on a sea-cliff or quarry. Feathery filmy leaves break

15  The pink *Erythronium revolutum* is an aristocrat for moist woodland soil. At Bulkeley Mill where this photograph was taken it has naturalized by the hundred.

16 *Colchicum
autumnale*—all the
colchicums are
good autumn-
flowering subjects
for the wild
garden. Asking
only to be left
alone they will
soon increase.

from the tall stems which bear cow-parsley-like heads of bright golden-yellow. There is also a purple-leafed form which is even more decorative.

**GALAX**
1½ ft × 1 ft
*Woodland*

*G. aphylla,* the Wand Flower, is a plant of great quality for good woodland conditions with cool, lime-free soil. It spreads slowly from its tufts of prettily rounded evergreen leaves which tint to red and copper in the winter. Its slender spikes of white flowers remind one of *Francoa ramosa,* the greenhouse Bridal Wreath.

**GERANIUM**
(spreading)
*Ground cover*

One of the very best and most attractive of all genera for efficient weed-suppression. Most species will thrive in any soil in sun or shade. Among the 'easies' are the bright pink *endressii,* the violet-blue *grandiflorum, ibericum platypetalum* of cottage gardens, the fine hybrid 'Johnson's Blue', *macrorrhizum* in pink or white, the tall blue *pratense* and its pink and silver cultivars., *sanguineum* and the native 'Bloody Cranesbill'. *Renardii* with its soft sage-green leaves and white flowers is also easy but more slow to increase. It is a pretty plant to lighten shady places. The beautiful *psilostemon* (*armenum*) with its large, elegant, deeply-cut leaves and brilliant magenta-crimson flowers will grow in sun or shade but needs good soil. The pretty *nodosum* with its cool lilac flowers is best in shade and appreciates a soil that is not too dry while the beautiful *wallichianum* 'Buxton's Blue' also enjoys shade. Not fully hardy everywhere this is the least reliable of the species mentioned.

**GUNNERA**
6 ft × 6 ft
*Waterside or Bog*

Too big for all but the largest wild gardens, *G. manicata* is a statuesque plant with deeply lobed, flat bristly leaves of six feet or more across. Not hardy in cold places where a cover-

K

ing of bracken or peat should be given in winter. Elsewhere the old leaves should be bent inwards to protect the furry crowns.

**HELLEBORUS**
$1\frac{1}{2}$–2 ft × 2 ft
*Ground cover.*
*Part shade*

Seeding freely many of the hellebores are first-rate plants for the wild garden. They will succeed almost anywhere but do best in partial shade. Untroubled by lime they will grow well on quarry or downs. Their main enemy is wind and for this reason they are best grown in the shelter of shrubs or hedgerow. *H. lividus* subsp. *corsicus* (*H. argutifolius*) with its heads of cupped chartreuse flowers and handsome spiny foliage is one of the most beautiful. The native *foetidus* is less splendid in leaf. Nevertheless it is early, easy and undemanding and its narrowly-fingered dark green leaves make an effective contrast with the apple-green cups that later become rimmed with brown. The Lenten roses, *H. orientalis* hybrids, have boldly fingered leaves and drooping, bowl-shaped heads in white, apple-blossom, pale green, peach, maroon and dusky plum-bloom often beautifully spotted within. A wide variation occurs from seed and to me, at any rate, they are endlessly beautiful and satisfying.

**HEMEROCALLIS**
2–3 ft × 2 ft
*Ground cover. Sun*
*or shade. Moist*
*soil*

The Day Lilies make fine clumps of strap-shaped leaves from which arise heads of lily-like flowers in primrose, gold, apricot, tan, copper, maroon, terra-cotta and near pink. Most are pleasing and the flowers open in succession over a long period. Any of the modern hybrids now offered will give satisfaction. When the soil is too dry they sometimes fail to flower.

**HERACLEUM**
10 ft × 6 ft
*Moist soil. Sun or*
*shade*

*H. mantegazzianum* is like a giant cow-parsley and is a large and very handsome plant for the wild garden. It is a perennial and will often seed itself—sometimes too freely—so that it

may be wiser to remove some of the heads before too much seed falls. Unfortunately it is too
big for small spaces and needs wind shelter on
account of its size.

**HEUCHERA**
1–2 ft × 2 ft
*Ground cover. Sun
or shade*

With spikes of airy flowers in shades of pink or
red arising from good basal clumps of pleasantly
shaped leaves the heucheras are useful ground
cover for sun or shade. × *Heucherella*—a
hybrid between this genus and that of tiarella is
even prettier but needs moist soil to do well.

**HOSTA**
2 ft × 1½ ft
*Moist soils. Sun or
shade*

A genus with handsome ribbed leaves that form
dense clumps thereby acting as weed-suppressors,
the hostas add interest to the wild garden and
their beautiful leaves are good for cutting. The
finest blue-leafed form is *sieboldiana*. There is
also a form of *fortunei* with steely-blue leaves
while the type has leaves of sage-green. *Albo-
marginata* has its leaves strikingly margined
with white while the young leaves of *fortunei*
'Albo-picta' are bright yellow margined with
pale green. Later by a gradual process the whole
of the leaf surfaces become green. A secondary
attraction are the spikes of lilac or lavender lily
flowers in late summer.

**IRIS**
Variable
*Conditions vary to
suit species*

Some of the finest decorative plants for the
waterside are to be found in this genus. Most
form dense rootstocks effectively keeping down
weeds. Among the best for the streamside, pool
margin or damp ground are the eighteen-inch
*chrysographes* with velvety black flowers in-
scribed with gold; the taller *sibirica* in white,
blue, purple or claret and the companionable
yellow *forrestii*; the later-flowering four-foot
× *monspur* 'Cambridge Blue', the soft yellow
× *ochraurea* and the white and yellow *ochroleuca*.
Also pleasing is the native yellow water-iris
*pseudacorus*, its paler variety *bastardii* and p.
'Variegata', a form with variegated leaves. For

dry ground the scented, pale lavender-blue *pallida dalmatica* is good with its handsome leaves while in rough ground anywhere *foetidissima* will enliven the autumn and winter with its handsome pods of orange berries. *Iris laevigata* in its various lovely forms will grow actually in the water while for moist ground anywhere I have always found the 'clematis-flowered' *kaempferi* much more accommodating than was formerly supposed. For winter beauty at the foot of an old wall or on a sunny ledge of rock *unguicularis* (*stylosa*) with its delicately lovely lavender flowers cannot be beaten.

**ISATIS**
3 ft × 2 ft
*Well-drained soil.*
*Sun*

The Woad, *I. tinctoria*, with which our early ancestors used to produce their war-paint dye is an attractive wild-garden plant, flowering in May with a cloud of filmy yellow tiny flowers. It is a biennial but one which seeds itself freely.

**KIRENGESHOMA**
3 ft × 2 ft
*Moist soils. Woodland*

*K. palmata* is a treasure for moist places in the woodland or near the waterside. It is alleged to need an acid soil. I have not tried it where lime is present so I cannot speak to the contrary and as its natural home is in acid soil in Japan I should imagine that is one of those plants the need of which for acid conditions is beyond dispute. With broad vine-like leaves of soft green and pale yellow shuttlecock flowers it is a lovely plant.

**KNIPHOFIA**
2–6 ft × 2 ft
*Sun. Good*
*drainage*

The red-hot pokers are striking plants for sunny, well-drained places. From the two-foot *galpinii* with its grey, grassy foliage and dainty apricot spires in October to the magnificent six-foot *nobilis* with its large scarlet 'pokers' all are effective. Even the common *uvaria* takes on a new stature and becomes beautiful beyond belief when seen against the blue sea as it lines a winding path leading down a wild cliff-garden. For those who like quieter colours the yellow 'Wrexham Buttercup' and white 'Maid of Orleans' are ideal.

**LAMIUM**
(spreading)
*Ground cover*

Combining beauty of foliage with its efficiency as a weed-suppressor the silver-variegated 'Yellow Archangel' *L. Galeobdolon* 'Luteum' (L. galeobdolon) is a dead-nettle of quality. It will succeed in poor dry soil or good, in sun or shade and is particularly effective when clothing a slope. More evergreen and just as dense a carpeter is the ubiquitous, creeping, purple-flowered *L. maculatum* with its silver-splashed, sage-green leaves that become tinged with pink in the winter. White- and pink-flowered forms also can be obtained and I have found them almost as reliable as the type. Unfortunately difficult to obtain, the comfortable *L. orvala* is an efficient summer ground cover although it dies down in winter. The white form is particularly good but both it and the red type make pleasantly bushy plants with soft green leaves and plump dead-nettle flowers. Whereas the other species are best increased by division *L. orvala* seeds itself and will also strike readily from cuttings.

**LAVATERA**
4 ft × 4 ft
*Sun. Poor soil*

*L. olbia* 'Rosea' is in fact semi-shrubby but I include it here because it is useful and colourful for a sunny place in poor or strong soil. It is short-lived but often seeds itself and can easily be renewed from hardwood cuttings taken with a heel in autumn or spring. Its large mallow-like flowers are freely borne and are a pale but pretty wash of mallow-purple in colour.

**LIGULARIA**
3–4 ft × 3 ft
*Damp Soil or*
*Waterside. Sun*

The ligularias are handsome plants for rich moist soil. *L. clivorum* in its varieties 'Othello' and 'Desdemona' is particularly fine with leathery leaves of verdigris green lined with rich claret purple. They are borne on foot-high stalks while the striking sprays of large orange daisy flowers rise to three or four feet. *L.* × *hessei* 'Gregynog Gold' is similar but the flowers instead of being carried in branching heads as in the *clivorum* varieties are borne in a broad, tapering spike. *L. veitchiana* has spikes of golden daisy flowers.

LINNAEA
(trailer)
*Woodland*

Beloved as the plant chosen by the great botanist Linnaeus to commemorate his name, the dainty northern Twin Flower *L. borealis* is a woodland treasure rather than a utility plant. With its tiny leaves and pairs of pale pink bells it is worth watching over and cherishing. It needs moist, woodsy acid soil to succeed.

LOBELIA
3 ft × 1 ft
*Sun or shade*
*Moist soil*

The tall blue *L. syphilitica* is an attractive late summer-flowering plant for moist soil or marshy ground near the waterside. I have found it reliably hardy even during severe winters. So, too, seems to be the crimson-purple *L. vedrariense*. Both are effective used in contrast with the *Ligularia clivorum* varieties.

LUNARIA
2 ft × 1 ft
*Sun or shade*

*L. biennis* (Honesty) is a useful self-sowing biennial colonizer for wild places with showy flowers like single-stocks in white, lavender and bright purple. The flowers are followed by the seed heads which, when their outer covering is shed, make the well-known silvery house decorations. There is also a white perennial species known as *L. rediviva*.

LUPIN
(variable)
*Sun. Ground cover*

The Tree Lupin *L. arborea* in sunny yellow, white or purple is a showy, sweet-scented plant for grass or poor, stony ground. It makes an effective ground cover and may be used to anchor sandy banks or dunes. Sometimes short-lived it nevertheless seeds itself freely and will establish colonies in suitably light soil. Some people use the ordinary herbaceous lupins as wild garden plants in orchards or grass but I much prefer to see the smaller, softer-coloured self-toned spikes of the tree varieties.

LUZULA
1 ft × 1 ft
(spreading)
*Ground cover.*
*Wood*

The wood-rush is a fine ground cover for difficult woodland slopes. It suppresses all weeds as it spreads, forming its dense grassy tussocks with their characteristic brown grass-flowers.

LYSICHITUM
3–4 ft × 3 ft
(spreading)
*Waterside. Weed*
*suppression*

Both the golden-spathed *L. americanum* with its huge, banana leaves in soft green and the cool white, blue-leafed *L. camtchatcense* are handsome waterside plants. Too invasive for narrow streams they are good in boggy ground or at the edge of large pools or wider stretches of water.

LYSIMACHIA
3 ft × 2 ft
*Ground cover. Sun*
*or shade*

Easy anywhere so long as the soil is not too dry, the lysimachias are useful as weed suppressors. Several species also have an appeal of their own. *Clethroides* with its curved buddleia-like white flower-heads and the golden *punctata* are among the best. All spread quickly into broad bands forming dense mats of roots through which no weeds can grow.

LYTHRUM
3 ft × 1 ft
*Any moist soil*

The Purple Loosestrifes are showy summer flowers for the wood, waterside, ditch or grass. 'The Beacon' (rosy-red), 'Brightness' (deep pink) and 'Dropmore Purple' are all good.

OENOTHERA
3 ft × 2 ft
*Any soil*

*O. lamarckiana* and *biennis* are splendid biennial species to naturalize in the wild garden. They will grow anywhere and are always welcome with their distinctive scent and luminous yellow flowers which open at dusk and remain open next day if the weather is dull.

OMPHALODES
½ ft × 1 ft
*Any good soil*

Two of the prettiest blue flowers of spring, *O. verna* and *O. cappadocica* will thrive in any soil that is not too dry. The sky blue *cappadocica* is perhaps the lovelier and needs shade to be seen at its best. *Verna* has gentian blue flowers that, like those of its sister species, are about the size of those of a forget-me-not; it runs more freely than *cappadocica* and is an effective ground cover.

ORIGANUM
½ ft × 1 ft
(spreading)
*Ground cover*

Best in sunny well-drained soil, *O. vulgare* 'Aureum' the golden-leafed marjoram is a gay little plant and a dense ground cover. Its leaves retain their golden hue until well into July.

PACHYSANDRA
¾ ft × 1 ft
(spreading)
*Ground cover*

*P. terminalis* is widely used in America as a ground cover for poor dry soil under trees. With dull, dark leaves it is not to my mind nearly as beautiful as periwinkle or ivy. There is, however, a variegated form marked with white at the edges of the leaves which will make a pleasant carpeter in a dark corner.

PAEONIA
(variable size)
*Good soil. Sun or*
*part shade*

Not for the rough and tumble of the purely functional wild garden but treasures for those wild gardeners who appreciate a good plant, some of the paeony species are effective in sheltered places. The shrubby *delavayi* (blood-red) and *lutea ludlowi* (yellow), the herbaceous *emodii* (milk white), *lactiflora* 'Whitleyi Major' (white), *mlokosewitschii* (yellow), *peregrina* (scarlet), *veitchii* (magenta) and its pink form *woodwardii* are all rewarding. None are difficult given good soil and shelter from cutting winds. The old double cottage garden paeonies are also pretty in orchard grass.

PELTIPHYLLUM
2 ft × 2 ft
*Wet ground*

Useful to bind streamside banks where the current is strong. *P. peltatum* is perhaps more familiar under it old name of *Saxifraga peltata*. Apart from its soil-holding properties, its main value lies in its large, foot-wide leaves which arise after the pink, starry flowers are done.

**PHLOMIS**
3 ft × 2 ft
*Ground cover. Sun. Any soil*

*P. samia* and *P. viscosa*, two soft-stemmed members of the Jerusalem Sage group are attractive sunny-looking plants for well-drained places in full sun. With characteristic whorls of hooded flowers in soft yellow above large leaves (very grey and woolly in the case of *samia*) they are handsome by any standards and the foliage is dense enough effectively to keep down weeds. Often *russelliana* is sent out instead of the above two species but all are good and make satisfactory wild garden plants.

**PODOPHYLLUM**
1½ ft × 1 ft
*Moist soil. Part shade*

The May Apple is a pleasing plant for moist woodland or for boggy ground. *P. emodii majus* is the species most readily obtainable and has prettily mottled, spreading chestnut-like leaves surmounted by apple-blossom cupped flowers, followed by shining scarlet fruits in late summer. It spreads slowly at the root.

**POLEMONIUM**
2–3 ft × 1 ft
*Will grow any-where*

Jacob's Ladder is the English name for these plants and refers to their attractive ferny, ladder-like leaves above which rise two- to three-foot stems bearing gold-centred heads of hyacinth-blue flowers. Graceful and pretty, they seed themselves and colonize readily, thriving anywhere—even in grass. *P. coeruleum* and its variety *richardsonii* are the best and easiest for the wild garden.

**POLYGONUM**
(varying heights)
*Sun. Ground cover*

A genus mainly of rampant weeds which contains also three good species for the wild garden. One of these is the native bistort, *P. bistorta* 'Superbum' with six- to nine-inch bottle-brush spikes of rose-pink above dense green leaves. This does best in reasonably good soil that is not too dry as does the tall and striking *P. amplexi-*

*caule* 'Atrosanguineum' which makes a dense leafy clump with narrow leaves and spikes of deep crimson flowers. *P. affine* is a ground-covering species for sunny places. Coming from Nepal it is not for the bleakest districts but south and west of the Trent it should be reliable in most gardens. It has spikes of deep pink flowers in late summer and forms a dense mat of narrow leaves which in autumn turn to deep russet. The form 'Darjeeling Red' has crimson flowers.

PRIMULA
(variable size)
*Sun or shade. Good soil*

One of the most useful genera for the wild garden. The charms of the primulas range from the wild primrose in its native sulphur and various coloured forms to the tall Asiatic species which must have good soil. Whereas the primrose does best in semi-shade in woodland or under hedges, the cowslip prefers chalky downland. Coloured varieties of both are available and the wild gardener should remember also the dainty Juliae varieties with their gay little flowers from claret to brick. Shades of blue and white are very attractive planted in little groups under shrubs or trees.

Of the candelabra primulas with whorls of flowers carried in tiers on taller stems, *japonica* (magenta, white or crimson), *pulverulenta* (a more refined magenta with mealy stems), *P.p.* 'Bartley Strain' in shades of pink, *bulleyana* (apricot), *chungensis* (orange) and *helodoxa* (yellow) are good. All need moist soil to grow in sun but if grown in shade will thrive in normal loam. I have not found them to mind the presence of lime in the soil although an acid soil is often advised. *Helodoxa* will stand a wetter place than the others as will the smaller, early bright pink *rosea* and the later pale yellow cowslip-flowered *sikkimensis* and *florindae*. Most inter-breed and all seed freely giving rise to pleasing colonies over the years. The good early-flowering drumstick-headed *denticulata* in shades of lavender and in white is also useful for damp places and will thrive in ordinary loam that is not too dry. Where the soil is very acid bonfire ash should be added to make it thrive.

**PULMONARIA**
¾ ft × 1 ft
(spreading)
*Ground cover*

All the Lungworts are excellent wild-garden plants. Earliest to flower—often in February—is the salmon-red *rubra*. Soon follows *officinalis* with large-spotted leaves and crozier heads of pink and blue giving rise to the country name of Soldiers and Sailors. There is a finer form known as 'Mrs. Moon' of the superior species *saccharata* with longer, tongue-shaped leaves more heavily marbled with the same blue-white spots as *officinalis*. Later to flower, the narrow-leafed *angustifolia azurea* is a startling beauty for shade with bright gentian-blue flowers. Less leafy, however, it is not such effective weed smother.

**RODGERSIA**
3–4 ft × 2 ft
*Ground cover.*
*Moist soil*

Handsome foliage plants with spiraea-like plumes of flower, the rodgersias are valuable for the waterside or moist ground. *R. aesculifolia* with bronzy horse-chestnut-like leaves and pale pink flowers, the deeper pink *pinnata* 'Superba' and white *tabularis* with big, flat almost circular leaves of rich velvety green are among the best.

**SALVIA**
1½–3 ft × 2 ft
*Ground cover. Sun*

The Sages are among the most useful plants for dry, stony soil. For the wild garden the best species are *haematodes* with flowers of lavender-blue, *sclarea*, *S.* var. *turkestanica* with beautiful grey leaves and soft pale blue flowers with pinky white bracts giving a soft and misty effect and the bright violet-blue × *superba*. The Common Sage in its red-leafed and variegated forms is also worth growing.

SCROPHULARIA
2 ft × 1 ft
*Ground cover.*
*Shade*

To lighten a dark place, *S. aquatica variegata*, the cream variegated form of a British weed is effective as ground cover and handsome in its own right.

SEDUM
1½–2 ft
*Sun. Good*
*drainage*

For awkward, dry, stony places the autumn-flowering sedums offer interest almost the year round with attractive fleshy leaves and late-summer to autumn colour. The various coloured forms of *S. spectabile* are all good with flat heads of tiny starry flowers in various shades of pink and red above blue-green leaves. For foliage contrast there are also *albo roseum* 'Variegatum'. its leaves variegated with creamy-yellow and *maximum* 'Atropurpureum' with rich maroon foliage.

SHORTIA
¾ ft × ¾ ft
(slowly spreading)
*Woodland*

Among the most beautiful of woodland treasures for special places *S. uniflora grandiflora* with fringed pale pink flowers and *S. galacifolia* with white flowers are not easy. They can be established successfully, however, if one can purchase good plants of three or four crowns which should be planted in shady woodland in sandy, leafy soil. *Galacifolia* is usually the easier of the two and it appreciates a diet of pine needles. In fact pine needles in the compost of either species is a considerable help towards success.

SMILACINA...
2½ ft × 1 ft
(spreading)
*Ground cover.*
*Damp woodland*

*Smilacina racemosa* is one of the most pleasant woodland plants with a delicious scent and the arching growth and leaves of Solomon's Seal but with fluffy spiraea-like flower plumes. Shade and damp leaf soil suit it well and it will slowly but surely spread to form a patch of good ground cover.

SYMPHYTUM
1–3 ft × 2 ft
(spreading) *Ground*
*cover. Any soil*

The dwarf *S. grandiflorum*, bearing little orange-tipped cream flowers in spring, is one of the most durable ground-covering plants with its mats of rough green leaves. Quickly spreading it will

foil all weeds and is especially useful in woodland or to prevent weeds invading cultivated
soil under shrubs. *S. peregrinum* is a three-foot
species forming large clumps but spreading by
seed. With hairy, coarse leaves and light blue
flowers carried in typical comfrey heads on
arching stems it is pleasing in the wild garden.

**TELLIMA**
2 ft × 1 ft
(spreading)
*Ground cover.*
*Shade*

Not unlike the heucheras but with pale green
flower spikes, *T. grandiflora* forms clumps of
rounded hairy leaves and spreads steadily. There
is a form of this species known as 'Purpurea'
with rich autumn effect and similar but more
yellowy flower spikes. The leaves of both last
throughout the winter except in very exposed
places.

**TIARELLA**
¾ ft × 1 ft
(spreading)
*Ground cover.*
*Shade*

Another of these very useful ground-covering
plants, *T. cordifolia* has pleasant heart-shaped
leaves and in spring puts up bottle-brush spikes
of foamy-white flowers thus earning its North
American name of Foam Flower. *T. wherryi*
is lovelier with tinted leaves and soft apricot,
scented spikes. It does not spread in the same
way, however, which changes its category from
that of the workaday, labour-saving carpeter to
that of an elegant treasure for special places
where it may effectively be used to complement
the primroses and dog-violets among the ivy of
the woodland floor.

**TRACHYSTEMON**
2 ft × 2 ft
*Ground cover. Any*
*soil*

Magnificent ground cover, seeding closely and
densely with huge softly hairy leaves and branching stems of curiously-shaped turquoise, borage
flowers.

**TRILLIUM**
¾–1½ ft × 1 ft
*Woodland*

The North American Wood Lilies are for
shady conditions in rich woodsy soil. *T. grandiflorum* with its large three-petalled white
flowers above threefold collars of handsome oval
leaves is the most pleasing. There are also

various striking erect-petalled species such as *sessile erectum* with maroon-purple cockades.

TROLLIUS
1½–2 ft × 1 ft
*Damp Soil or waterside*

From the pale butter balls of the native *T. europaeus* of our northern riversides and water meadows to the orange-gold of the newer hybrids, the Globe Flowers are good value for the wild garden. Not absolutely dependent on boggy conditions to survive both *T. europaeus* and the later-flowering 'Orange Queen' and similar hybrids will grow equally well in woodland, orchard or meadow-grass provided the soil is reasonably moist.

UVULARIA
1 ft × 1 ft
*Shady woodland*

A small Solomon's Seal-like woodlander of character with graceful stems and drooping bells of pale yellow.

VERBASCUM
2–6 ft × 1–2 ft
*Sun*

The verbascums are stately plants for sun and poor soil. They do well on limestone and chalk but will grow in any open, sunny place. Among the best perennial species are *V. chaixii (vernale)* with basal rosettes of large grey leaves and five-foot branching candelabra spikes of yellow, *olympicum* with handsome felted leaves and six-foot spires of yellow, and *thapsiforme* with deep crinkly leaves and branching spikes four to five feet. Of the hybrids reliable varieties are 'Cotswold Beauty' (biscuit), 'Cotswold Gem' (peach), 'Cotswold Queen' (amber), 'Gainsborough' (yellow) and 'Pink Domino'. The handsome *V. bombyciferum* (broussa) is a biennial which can be relied on to perpetuate itself by seeding. With its heavy silver basal rosettes and woolly six-foot spikes of bright golden yellow it is a rewarding plant for any garden.

VINCA
(trailing)
*Ground cover. Any soil*

Although botanically classed as shrubs, most gardeners think of periwinkles as among the carpeting section of lowly ground-cover plants and for that reason I include them here. Where large areas are to be covered, the eighteen-inch *V. major*, with its arching, rooting stems of shiny dark green leaves and large flowers of periwinkle-blue, is ideal. It is also good to cover a rough bank or mingled with ivy on the woodland floor to act as a carpeter for primroses, snowdrops, hardy cyclamen and similar treasures. *V. minor* is smaller in all its parts but if clipped back after flowering it makes a dense ground cover. Both species may be used to hold soil on steep banks or in other difficult places. There is a fine cream-variegated form of *major* also an attractive narrow-petalled form *acutiloba* with flowers of deeper violet and a winter-flowering species for sheltered places *difformis* with starch-white flowers that become pale blue with the coming of spring. Of *minor* there are forms with silver and golden variegations and also a white-flowered variety, two different blues (both excellent), a wine purple and also double-flowered forms in blue and claret.

**VIOLA**
(carpeter)
*Shade. Woodsy soil*

All the violets are pretty in the wild garden to grow on hedgebanks, around orchard trees or under shrubs. In their own modest way they make effective ground cover. Even the dog violet is worth encouragement and the sweet-scented varieties of *odora* in purple, blue, pink, white, sulphur and wine are a delight. The dark-leaved *labradorica* is an attractive carpeter. There is the taller *septentrionalis* with large flowers of white and violet and on moorland in sandy places and sometimes along hedgerows the native *lutea* and *tricolor* will succeed and offer an enchanting variety of tiny pansy faces.

# Reliable Shrubs for Ground Cover in the Wild Garden

**CALLUNA** (Ling)
1–2 ft × 1 ft
(spreading)
*Acid soil*

Recommended varieties: 'Alportii' (tall crimson), 'Alportii praecox', 'County Wicklow' (double lilac dwarf), 'Cuprea' (golden foliage in summer, copper in winter), 'Hammondii' (tall white), 'Hammondii Aurea' (white with golden foliage ),'H. E. Beale' (fine double lilac, late-flowering), 'Mair's White', 'Ruth Sparkes', (double white), 'J. H. Hamilton' (dwarf, double rose), 'Joan Sparkes' (double pink).

**CISTUS**
3–5 ft × 4 ft
*Sun. Good
    drainage*

Many of the cistus are not sufficiently hardy to be recommended as ground cover but × *loretii* is. Making a mounded two-foot bush its skirts hug the ground closely. It is attractive at all times of the year with pleasant dark green glaucous leaves. Its flowering period is a long one and often in autumn it will carry a second crop of its large white flowers with their crimson basal blotches. Another hardy hybrid cistus is × *corbariensis* with dark green narrow leaves, reddish stems and crinkly white gold-centred flowers.

**COTONEASTER**
(horizontal
    varieties)

*C. adpressus praecox* (Nan Shan) deciduous, similar to *horizontalis* in its arching growth but with larger, orange-red berries. Autumn leaf

1–2 ft × 3–6 ft
or more
*Any soil*

colour. *C. conspicuus decorus* is evergreen, of mounded spreading growth up to two feet high or a little more. Bright red berries. Excellent for covering banks and like the ubiquitous, deciduous *horizontalis* a useful retainer of soil with its widely-spreading fibrous roots. The evergreen *microphyllus* is one of the best of the section to provide winter furnishing for the wild garden or rock face with its dense drapery of branches. Thickly covered with small dark leaves and large red berries. *Dammeri* is another evergreen species, forming mats of shining leaves, but its berries are not so well displayed.

CYTISUS
*Sun*

There are several dwarf brooms which combine a showy flower display with effective ground cover. For pure chalk the genista section are more reliable although the cytisus succeed in all other soils including the carboniferous lime-stones of the Midlands and the North-West. The hybrids × *beanii* (gold) and × *kewensis* (cream) are excellent and may be used along with the purple-flowered *purpureus* and its white variety *albus*. Also good are the taller, creamy *praecox* of fountain-like growth, *C.p. alba* (white), 'Hillieri' (buff-apricot) and the pink 'Hollandia'.

DABOECIA
½ ft × 2–3 ft
*Acid soil*

The Irish Heath with its large urn-shaped flowers conspicuously held on their wiry stalks and neat dark foliage is a striking ground cover shrublet for acid soil. The most striking forms are *D. cantabrica*, 'Alba', 'Atropurpurea' and 'Praegerae'.

ELAEAGNUS
3 ft × 4–5 ft
*Sun. Good
    drainage*
L

*E. macrophylla* is an attractive sprawling ground-cover shrub for sunny places or well-drained banks. Its broad silvery, rippling leaves make dense cover and when established it bears in November delightfully-scented tiny silver fuchsia-like flowers.

ERICA
¾–5 ft × 1–4 ft

One section of this useful carpeting genus will succeed on limy soils. They are the *E. carnea* varieties. The autumn-flowering *terminalis* (*stricta*) (3–4 ft) and the spring-blooming *mediterranea* and its hybrid × *darleyensis* will also tolerate limy conditions. It is safer to assume that all other species need acid soil. Good varieties of the winter-flowering *carnea* species are 'Springwood White' (Jan.-Feb.) and the earlier-blooming 'Cecilia M. Beale'. Pink and carmine varieties to give a long succession of colour are 'King George', 'White Beauty', 'Praecox', 'Ruby Glow', 'Springwood Pink', 'James Backhouse' and 'Thomas Kingscote'. The hybrid × *darleyensis* and its improved forms 'A. T. Johnson' and the fine 'George Rendall' give greater height and long flower sprays.

For acid soils good early summer-flowering *cinerea* varieties (our native bell-heather) are: 'Alba Major', 'Atropurpurea', 'Atrorubens', 'C. D. Eason' (pink), 'Golden Hue' and 'Apple Blossom'. The Cornish heath *E. vagans* with its sturdy bottle-brush flower spikes is, in my experience, more tolerant of lime. Varieties to choose include 'Mrs. Maxwell' (fine bright rose), 'Pyrenees Pink', 'Lyonesse' (white) and 'Alba Superba'.

There is also *E. ciliaris*, the Dorset Heath, with its varieties, while *E. tetralix*, the Cross-Leafed Heath, has several colourful cultivars, some named after the various members of the Underwood family, and a good white with frosty emerald foliage, *E.t. alba mollis*. Taller growing but densely furnished to the ground so as to completely eliminate weeds are the spring-flowering rosy-red *E. mediterranea* (3 ft) and its lower-growing varieties 'Brightness' and the very early excellent white 'W. T. Rackliff'. Still taller and a little later to bloom is the Fox Tailed Tree Heath *lusitanica* with its characteristic growth and scented pink-tinged ash-white small bells. This is not, however, hardy in cold gardens nor is its hybrid × *veitchii*, nor the large-belled rosy *australis*, nor the white *australis* 'Mr. Robert'. *E. arborea alpina* is the hardiest of the tree-heaths with mossy green foliage and ash-white bells making a dense broadly-based bush of four feet high.

**ESCALLONIA**
3–4 ft × 4–5 ft
*Any soil. Sun*

Three of the escallonias are hardy and reliable enough to use as ground cover, forming mounded bushes, furnished to the ground with arching growths and bearing in summer and autumn sprays of pretty red or pink flowers. 'William Watson' (red), × *langleyensis* (rose-crimson) and × *edinensis* (rose-pink) are the ones to choose.

**EUONYMUS**

(The species mentioned may be grown as carpeters or climbers.)
*E. fortunei* (*radicans*) offers two varieties that are particularly attractive to cover a rock-face or bank or to be used as prostrate ground cover in sun or shade. *E.r.* 'Coloratus' has small pretty leaves that become splashed and tinted with claret in the winter, while 'Silver Queen' has daintily pointed leaves variegated with cream that are often tinged with pink in the winter. There is also the useful dwarf species *E. nanus* which is a good soil retainer and cover for banks.

**GAULTHERIA**
½–3 ft
(spreading)
*Acid soil*

Doing best in a moist, lime-free soil in partial shade, the gaultherias are mostly runners affording good, dense ground cover, neat evergreen leaves, heath-like flowers and pretty berries. Good species for the average wild garden are the little creeping *itoana* with bright red berries, the slightly taller (9-inch) *miqueliana* with white berries and the close-carpeting red-berried *procumbens*. G. *shallon* grows to four or five feet high in shade and making impenetrable thickets is ideal to cover a large area of rough ground. It is not to be trusted near smaller treasures. The bigeneric hybrid × *Gaulthettya wisleyensis* is good and less invasive with its pernettya-like habit and heavy crops of blood-red berries.

GENISTA
(Recommended
dwarf species
mainly pros-
trate)
*Sun*

Allied to the brooms, these genistas offer showy golden flowers allied to dense ground cover. Among the most useful are the winged *januensis*, *sagittalis* and *tinctoria* 'Flore Pleno'. The taller *lydia* with its swirls of arching branches remains densely furnished to the ground and is a most attractive shrub.

× HALIMIOCISTUS
1 ft × 2 ft
*Sun. Good
drainage*

Similar to their cistus parent the × *Halimiocistus* are dwarfer. × *H. sahucii* is the hardiest and is a very pleasant ground-covering shrub with dark green branches and crinkly white, gold-bossed flowers. Halimium, one of the parent genera, has in *ocymoides* a bright yellow-flowered sun rose with chocolate blotches on the flowers and neat grey leaves. It makes dense mounds of two or three feet in height.

HYPERICUM
½–3 ft × 2–3 ft
*Sun or shade*

One of the finest soil-retaining species for difficult banks is the prostrate spreading *calycinum*, the Rose of Sharon, with its wide golden saucers. Rather taller at eighteen-inches high is *moserianum* which makes shapely dense ground-covering mounds, covered with similarly large

golden flowers. More shrubby, making three-
to five-foot bushes in time but always staying
dense to the ground is the excellent *H. patulum*
'Hidcote'.

**JUNIPERUS**
(spreading)
*Any soil*

The junipers are among the best of evergreen
ground covers, thriving in poor soil or covering
banks. They will even grow in the direct blast
of the sea wind where most other conifers are
turned brown or killed. *J. chinensis sargentii* is
a pretty, prostrate species with light green young
foliage and glaucous adult leaves. *J. communis
prostrata* is a good mat-forming variety. *J.
horizontalis* is one of the best to cover wide
areas, spreading fairly quickly with blue-green
leaves. There are several forms which take on
deep steely blue or purple tints in winter. *J.* ×
*media* 'Pfitzeriana' is taller in growth reaching
to five feet or more in time and having a spread
of eight feet—'Aurea', 'Armstrongii', 'Glauca'
and 'Glauca plumosa' are good colour forms of
this species. *J. sabina* 'Arcadia' is a glaucous,
low-growing ground-covering form while *J.s.*
'Scandens' and the well-known 'Tamariscifolia' are also effective near-prostrate cultivars.

**KALMIA**
2–6 ft × 6 ft
*Acid soil*

For acid woodland or heathland the kalmias are
pretty summer-flowering shrubs with a different look. With neat evergreen leaves and small,
pucker-mouthed buds that open like little para-
chutes. *K. augustifolia* is the smaller of the two
species and is thicket-forming to three feet high
with narrow leaves and rosy-red flowers. *K a.*
'Rubra' is a deeper-coloured form. *K. latifolia*
has broader leaves and warm pink flowers. Both
are easy in good rhododendron soil and will
grow in sun as well as shade provided the soil
is sufficiently moist.

LAVANDULA
1–3 ft × 1–3 ft
*Sun*

For poor stony soils and dry banks the lavenders are easy and characterful ground-cover shrubs. 'Munstead Dwarf', 'Twickel Purple', 'Hidcote', 'Hidcote Pink', 'Grappenhall', *spica*, *spica alba* and *vera* are all good. The maquis lavender, *L. stoechas*, is striking and uncommon with chunky, cockaded heads of dark purple. It is not hardy in bleak districts but for a sea-cliff or quarry in a sheltered district it is ideal.

LITHOSPERMUM
(prostrate,
    spreading)
*Sun*

With their brilliant blue flowers and neat ever-green leaves the lithospermums are most desir-able garden plants. *L. diffusum* in the forms 'Grace Ward' and 'Heavenly Blue' needs a moist cool root run and an acid soil. It will succeed on sandstone rocks or may be used to make a striking splash of colour at the fore-front of heaths. On chalk or limestone places the allied *Moltkia petraea* is more reliable.

MAHONIA
(Dwarf species
    range from
    1–3 ft.
    Spreading)
*Any Soil*

*M. aquifolium* is surely one of the best known of all shrubs for underplanting and is a most useful species spreading well with its running, rooting stems and handsome pinnate leaves leaves which often colour well in winter—par-ticularly when grown in sun. The fat, short racemes of bright yellow flowers are pleasant in spring and are followed by blue-black berries. *M. nervosa* is another running species with longer, thinner leaves and slightly larger racemes. *M. repens rotundifolia* is also useful and a little later flowering with deeper yellow flower spikes and blue-green, spineless leaves. All are fine in woodland, heath, grass, on dry banks where they help to retain the soil or even on quarry ledges or cliffs. They are among the most useful of wild garden plants.

**PERNETTYA**
3 ft
(spreading)
*Peaty or woodland soil*

Allegedly lime-hating, I have found the pernettyas successful on moist, humus-laden alkaline soil. I think it is the humus-content that is all-important. Planted at two feet apart the pernettyas will sucker freely to form a dense mass of dark prickly leaves. Their white flowers are urn-shaped and heathlike and followed in autumn by marble-sized berries in white, pink, lilac, crimson or claret. One or two males should be included in the planting to ensure free-fruiting. One of the best ground-covering shrubs for winter effect.

**PHLOMIS**
Hardy
2–3 ft × 2–4 ft
*Sun. Good drainage*

Except in the coldest places *Phlomis fruticosa* the Jerusalem Sage is a splendid grey-leafed shrub to cover a sunny bank. It may be used also in the heath or downland garden where it will make a useful contrast plant, or it may be used to form a ground-smothering *maquis* in conjunction with cistuses, lavenders, rosemary and other sun-loving shrubs. Its large golden-hooded flowers are sage-like in shape and borne in whorls.

**PHORMIUM**
3–9 ft × 2 ft
*Sun*

The sword-like leaves of *P. tenax* the New Zealand Flax are evergreen and useful for foliage effect in dry, sunny places. They are in keeping in a cliff or quarry garden and are striking in the foreground of a *maquis* planting such as that just described. *P.t.* 'Veitchii' has its leaves handsomely striped with yellow.

**POTENTILLA**
1–6 ft × 3 ft
*Any soil. Sun or shade*

Although they are not evergreen the dwarf members of this genus are densely furnished with ground-hugging branches and make useful ground cover during the summer months. With prettily divided leaves and large strawberry flowers in white or yellow they are attractive enough to use anywhere in the wild garden. The varieties and species mentioned flower over a long period: *P. arbuscula* (shaggy brown branches and large golden flowers), *fruticosa* 'Beesii' (low silver hummocks with golden flowers), 'Elizabeth' (gold), *farreri* (gold), *mandschurica* (white flowers, grey leaves and purple stems—mat-forming), 'Manelys' (soft yellow).

RHODODENDRON (dwarf and hybrid species)
*Acid soil*

Including the azaleas, this genus offers among its dwarfs some most attractive plants for dense, low ground-cover in acid soil. Unlike the larger species and hybrids these dwarfs do not need shade and in fact do better in open airy positions. They are admirable in a heath garden and with their sturdier growth and varying leaf colour add interest and texture. The members of the Lapponicum series are particularly useful to form close carpeted drifts with colourful flower effect in spring, often followed by a second but more limited flowering in autumn and with winter leaf colours of bronze, frosty grey, verdigris, near blue and light and dark greens. A good selection would include *chryseum* (yellow), *microleucum* (white), *lysolepis* (rosy purple), *intricatum* and *impeditum* (harebell blue) and *scintillans* (near sapphire). These might merge into the various scarlet *forrestii* var. *repens* hybrids with their more leathery leaves such as the prostrate 'Elizabeth' clone 'Jenny' and 'Little Ben' and the *williamsianum* hybrids such as 'Treasure' (pink,) 'Moonstone' (pink-rimmed cream) and 'Humming Bird' (cerise). Also useful are the blue-flowered hybrids loosely classed as Lapponicum hybrids such as 'Blue Diamond', 'Augfast', 'Sapphire' and the violet 'Prostigiatum'. The *scintillans* × *calostrotum* hybrid 'Pink Drift' in its best pink forms is also good.

Similar but more brilliant effects may be obtained by the use of the dwarf evergreens of the Azalea section. Some of the Kurume azaleas are too harsh in colour for extensive use in the wild garden but selective plantings of softer shades such as 'Kirin' (pink), 'Iro-hayama' (lavender), 'Kure-no-yuki' (white) and 'Azuma-Kagami' (deep pink) are pleasant to look at. Most attractive are the large-flowered white *mucronatum* and its lilac and pink-striped white forms. These will thrive even in grass and are pretty and most effective near a stream.

**ROSMARINUS**
(prostrate—6 ft
   Dense to the
      ground
*Sun. Good
   drainage*

The early *lavandulaceus* (*prostratus*) is not fully hardy. However it is lovely for draping rocks or clothing a sunny slope in milder districts or by the sea. The bright-blue-flowered 'Severn Sea' is a remarkably hardy form of *R. officinalis* making compact low mounds. The beautiful 'Tuscan Blue' and 'Benenden Blue' are only hardy enough for sheltered warm places or seaside use.

**RUBUS**
1–6 ft
(sprawling)
*Shade*

Many of the garden brambles like the rest of their family have thorns that are a menace. They will, however, grow where little else will do so, are decorative and will make useful ground cover. Among the best is the thornless *R. deliciosus* with large rose-like white flowers in May, the prostrate, creeping evergreen *fockeanus* which forms a dense mat of attractive foliage, *nobilis* with bright red-purple flowers, *spectabilis* with rosy-magenta flowers, the very bristly but thornless *tricolor* with shiny green leaves, white-felted on the underside. The beautiful hybrid 'Tridel' with its three-inch white flowers and *ulmifolius bellidiflorus* with double rose-pink flowers are taller, arching shrubs which may be placed as one would place a species rose in grass or woodland in any part of the wild garden.

RUSCUS
2 ft
(spreading)
*Any soil*

The Butcher's Broom is a pleasant wild garden shrub for winter with its odd dark green spiny cladodes and bright red berries. It will grow anywhere in sun or shade and will thrive in the poorest soil. To obtain berries it is best to plant the hermaphrodite form or to ensure that bushes of both sexes are established.

SALIX
Dwarf species
1–3 ft
(spreading)
*Any soil*

One of the most useful dwarf willows for ground cover is the native *repens* often used to hold the sand in coastal districts. Running rapidly it colonizes a good area and is pretty in spring with its comparatively large fluffy yellow catkins. There is a taller form with silvery leaves known as *S.r. argentea* which makes arching mounds of growth up to three feet high. Another handsome species is the woolly *lanata*, growing eventually to two or three feet. It needs more soil than *repens* and will do well on moorland or downs. Also attractive but miniature-tree-like rather than spreading are the pretty *apoda* in which the female catkins are grey and the male pink and orange, the Chinese *bockii* which bears its catkins in autumn and the hybrid × *boydii* which grows to only a foot. Making a close six-inch mat the native *herbacea* is a useful plant for banks.

SARCOCOCCA
1–4 ft
(thicketing)
*Shade. Good soil*

The sarcococcas are dwarf suckering shrubs with neat glossy evergreen foliage. They bear tiny puffs of sweetly-scented flowers in winter. The foot-high *humilis* is one of the best for ground cover. The taller *S. ruscifolia* grows to four feet and there is also *hookeriana digyna* with slightly larger flowers.

SENECIO
2–3 ft × 3–6 ft
*Sun. Good
    drainage*

Attractive grey-leafed shrubs of dense spreading habit that are well able to withstand wind, the senecios are particularly useful for coastal and downland gardens. *S. compactus* is the most dwarf at two feet, *laxifolius* and *greyi* are both good with sunny yellow daisy flowers above their rounded silver-felted leaves. *S. monroi* is attractive and free-flowering with deeper yellow daisies and pleasing crinkle-edged leaves.

**SPIRAEA**
Dwarf species
*Any soil*

The two-foot *S. bumalda* is a pleasant deciduous shrub with thicketing stems making pleasant summer ground cover. It will grow in grass or on a sunny bank and is generally easy and accommodating. The type has flat heads of deep pink flowers. In 'Anthony Waterer' they are crimson. An attractive cream and pink variegation of foliage appears in a number of forms and seems to occur especially when they are growing in well-drained places.

**STRANVAESIA**
Dwarf species
*Any soil*

A form of *S. davidiana*—*S.d. undulata* is of spreading low growth and useful to cover a bank or slope. The dark green leaves are evergreen and acquire scarlet and orange tints in winter. Bright red berries are borne by the type and there is also a variety with yellow berries known as 'Fructu Luteo'.

**ULEX**
1–4 ft
*Any soil except*
    *shallow chalk*

One of the most useful and attractive of our native ground-covering plants the golden gorse is excellent to retain soil and cover awkward slopes. It makes bold splashes of colour in the heathland garden or on a cliff or rock face. The common gorse *U. europaeus* reaches to four feet or so and will seed freely but seedlings are prickly and when established difficult to uproot so where self-sown clumps are not wanted the double-flowered form *E.e.* 'Flore Pleno' should be used instead. *U. gallii* and *nanus* are dwarfer species which tend to flower more in autumn and are good to cover stretches among heaths or to plant at the forefront of shrubs.

VACCINIUM
½–6 ft
(spreading)
*Acid soil*

The Bilberry is often used as a ground-cover plant. The North American *V. corymbosum* is one of the best dual-purpose vacciniums— named varieties yielding large and luscious blueberries and at the same time being attractive in leaf and flower and colouring well in autumn before the leaves drop. The cranberry *V. macrocarpum* is a prostrate evergreen species, spreading rapidly with small pink flowers and luscious scarlet berries. *V. myrtillus* is the native bilberry of the moors and *V. vitis-idaea*—a foot-high creeping shrub and another native—is an evergreen species making good ground cover. Of the taller species the evergreen four-foot *glauco-album* is one of the best with pale pink flowers and blue-white bloom covering the fruits, bracts and under-surfaces of the leaves.

VIBURNUM
Dwarf species
    may be used
*Any soil*

*V. davidii* is the species most often used for ground cover. It is a pleasing mounded two-foot shrub with leathery, oval ribbed leaves. Male and female plants are required to produce the brilliant turquoise berries.

YUCCA
3–6 ft × 2–3 ft
*Sun. Good
    drainage*

Useful accent plants and ground cover for dry sunny places with handsome sword-like leaves and tall spikes of creamy lily flowers. *Y. filamentosa recurvifolia* and *glauca* are satisfactory and free-flowering species to grow. The magnificent *gloriosa* is not so reliable in flower but is worth growing for the architectural quality of its leaves. The flower spikes when borne are especially striking, the inflorescence being as much as four feet in length.

# Ferns for the Wild Garden
## (Ground Cover and Decorative)

**ADIANTUM**
1½ ft
*Wind shelter*

The Hardy Maidenhair Fern *A. pedatum* may need a protective mulch of dry bracken in cold areas. It will succeed quite easily, however, in most gardens where it can be given a sheltered position among shrubs and is worth a place where its lovely soft green fronds and wiry black stems will not be blasted by the wind.

**ASPLENIUM**
1 ft
*Rocks*

*A. trichomanes*, the Maidenhair Spleenwort, is a pretty and easily grown little fern to tuck into wall crannies or crevices in rock. It is like a tiny Maidenhair Fern in appearance.

**ATHYRIUM**
2–3 ft × 1 ft
*Moist soil. Part shade*

*A. filix-femina*, the Lady Fern, makes dense clumps of fine lacy green fronds and is a splendid plant for ground cover in any reasonable moist soil. There are various crested varieties available for special places in the wild garden where their detailed charms can be admired.

**BLECHNUM**
2 ft
(spreading)
*Moist soil. Sheltered*

Formerly known as *Lomaria magellanica*, *B. tabulare* is a handsome exotic fern that is hardy in many districts provided it is given woodland conditions with an overhead canopy of branches to protect from frost. A winter mulch of bracken or straw will ensure its safety in cold districts. It needs moist soil and is effective near water where it is very handsome with its wide fronds and broad leaflets of full, warm green.

**DRYOPTERIS**
2½–3 ft
*Any soil. Shade*

Two very vigorous ground-covering species are among this genus—*D. dilatata* and *D. filix-mas*. *D. dilatata* the Broad Buckler Fern is a sturdy rich green fern with broad-based, rather triangular fronds. The Marsh Buckler Fern, *D. thelypteris*, is especially useful for wet ground. It will grow even in the water, sending out its creeping rootstocks over a wide area. The two-foot fronds are more slender and dainty than those of the Broad Buckler Fern and rise singly from along the rootstock. The Male Fern, *D. filix-mas*, is another easy and handsome fern to naturalize in any shady place, or even on dry ground, with lance-shaped fronds of deep green. There are many beautiful crested forms and and it is evergreen in many places.

**MATTEUCCIA**
3 ft
*Moist loamy soil*

*M. struthiopteris*, the Ostrich Feather Fern is one of the most distinctive and beautiful of all hardy ferns. It will grow in any moist or even boggy ground and is particularly attractive at the waterside. Increasing well it makes first-class ground cover.

**ONOCLEA**
1–1½ ft
*Moist ground or waterside*

*O. sensibilis* is another lovely and distinctive species for growing by the waterside or in moist woodland. Single, broad, deeply-segmented fronds arise from the creeping rootstock. It will grow in any soil that does not dry out too much and makes first-class ground cover.

**OSMUNDA**
3–6 ft
*Good moist loam or waterside*

The Royal Fern, *O. regalis*, is the largest and most magnificent of hardy ferns with immense graceful fronds, deep green in summer and russet-tinted as they unroll in spring. It is splendid in a damp ditch or near water.

**PHYLLITIS**
1 ft
*Any soil*

The Hart's Tongue Fern, *P. scolopendrium*, is one of the best loved and most attractive of native ferns with its undivided, strap-shaped fronds. In the wild it is often found on limestone but it will grow anywhere, even where the soil is dry and makes a useful contrast to other plants in the wild garden. There are forms with wavy and with crested fronds.

**POLYPODIUM**
1–1½ ft

*P. dryopteris* (1 ft) the Oak Fern and *P. vulgare* the Common Polypody are extremely easy and accommodating creeping ferns sending up their apple-green fronds from a creeping rootstock and growing even on dry banks and the tops of walls. It is characterful and dense but does not afford the luxuriant cover of athyrium or dryopteris.

**POLYSTICHUM**
2 ft
*Any soil*

The Hard Shield Fern, *P. aculeatum*, is a distinctive native fern with lacy, much-divided long yellow-green fronds that are carried almost horizontally. An even more elegant allied species *P. setiferum densum* has very fresh green much-divided fronds. Both are evergreen in most winters and increase slowly to form good ground cover.

꿗

# Additional Tree Suggestions
## for the Wild Garden

彡彡彡

### For Year-Round Beauty

ABIES FORRESTII (Silver Fir with blue violet cones), ABIES CONCOLOR VIOLACEA (glaucous form of Colorado Fir).

ACER GRISEUM (tattered cinnamon bark Maple), ACER GROSSERII HERSII (striated green and white bark Maple).

ARBUTUS ANDRACHNE (mild areas), × ANDRACHNOIDES and MENZIESII (cinnamon or tan bark, evergreen).

BETULA ALBO-SINENSIS SEPTENTRIONALIS (orange-brown-barked birch), B. JACQUEMONTII (creamy bark, coloured almost to tips of young shoots), B. PAPYRIFERA (white).

CEDRUS ATLANTICA GLAUCA (beautiful blue Cedar—only for large spaces).

CHAMAECYPARIS LAWSONIANA 'Erecta Viridis' (bright green upright False Cypress), C. L. 'Stewartii' (fine gold), 'Triomphe de Boskoop' (one of the best blue forms), C. L. 'Wisselii' (narrowly upright form of distinct appearance).

EUCALYPTUS GUNNII, URNIGERA and PERRINIANA (beautiful reasonably hardy eucalypti with fine bark and blue-grey leaves—evergreen. Must be planted in spring).

GINKGO BILOBA (deciduous broad-leafed conifer with beautiful leaves shaped like a maidenhair fern. Fine autumn colour).

JUNIPERUS VIRGINIANA (the Pencil Cedar with peeling bark and grey-green foliage).

LIRIODENDRON TULIPIFERA (magnificent deciduous Tulip Tree with handsome foliage).

NOTHOFAGUS DOMBEYI and BETULOIDES (handsome evergreen Southern Beeches for the milder counties).

PICEA BREWERIANA (the Weeping Spruce), P. OMORIKA (fine hardy Spruce), P. PUNGENS 'Kosteriana' (Blue Colorado Spruce, one of the 'bluest' of all conifers).

PINUS AYACAHUITE (fine hardy Pine), P. PINEA (the Stone Pine of the Mediterranean with its characteristic wide top and low stature. Must have good soil and be planted in fairly frost-free sites), P. RADIATA (formerly INSIGNIS, the Monterey Pine, only suitable for sea-side districts where it is very fine with rich green foliage and handsome four-inch cones).

PRUNUS SERRULA TIBETICA (polished-barked Cherry).

### For Spring Blossom

MALUS × FLORIBUNDA (the weeping Japanese Crab with apple-blossom flowers in early May), 'John Downie' (white blossom—large orange and scarlet fruit in Autumn), 'Profusion' (a good wine-red with coppery young leaves), 'Simcoe' (rose-pink flowers followed by red and yellow fruit).

PRUNUS, the Ornamental Cherries, may be divided into: Early Singles: 'Okamé', 'Kursar' and SARGENTII (rosy pinks), YEDOENSIS (very graceful blush). The Large-flowered Japanese Cultivars: 'Fugenzo' (pink), 'Ukon' (primrose), 'Mikurumagaeshi' (pink upright), 'Amanogawa' (the pale pink maypole fastigiate cherry), 'Kanzan' (very vigorous bright pink), 'Tai Haku' (immense-flowered white single), 'Shirotae' (lovely double white), 'Shimidsui' (long-stalked pretty frilly white), 'Jo-nioi' (single flowered, fragrant white), 'Shiro-fugen' (blush pink).

### For Early Summer Bloom

CERCIS SILIQUASTRUM (the Judas Tree with rosy purple pea flowers wreathing the bare stems in May).

M

CORNUS NUTTALLII (a beautiful Dogwood with cream-bracted rounded 'flowers' in May) C. KOUSA CHINENSIS (four-bracted strikingly angular 'flowers' in June).

CRATAEGUS OXYACANTHA (the Hawthorn—one of our prettiest native trees in double white, double and single pink and double and single scarlet).

DAVIDIA INVOLUCRATA (the Handkerchief Tree with large ghost-like six-inch bracts in May).

HALESIA CAROLINA (a Snowdrop Tree with a profusion of pendent white bells in May).

MAGNOLIA × HIGHDOWNENSIS (summer-flowering magnolia for chalk with pendent, bowl-shaped, scented flowers), M. SIE-BOLDII (more sprawling in habit), M. WILSONII (more tree like and takes longer to mature), M. × WATSONII (glorious tree-like magnolia with ivory-cream, crimson bossed, solid textured saucer-flowers).

STYRAX HEMSLEYANA, JAPONICA and OBASSIA (beautiful June-flowering Snowdrop Trees for woodland conditions).


## For Late Summer Flowers

AESCULUS × CARNEA (Red Horse Chestnut), A. PAVIA (smaller growing red-flowered species).

EUCRYPHIA GLUTINOSA (deciduous species for acid soil with beautiful white Rose-of-Sharon flowers with a freckling of red-brown anthers and fine autumn colour), E. × NYMANSAY (tall, columnar evergreen species. Less striking perhaps in flower but longer lasting).

STEWARTIA PSEUDO-CAMELLIA and S. SINENSIS (graceful small deciduous trees with fine autumn colour and cup-shaped white flowers in July and August. Sunny woodland position with moist soil or in more open settings among dwarf heaths which will shade their roots).

## For Autumn Beauty

ACER PALMATUM and varieties (wind shelter. Fine leaf colour).

CERCIDIPHYLLUM JAPONICUM (heart-shaped leaves. Colours best near water in very moist soil).

LIQUIDAMBAR STYRACIFLUA (brilliant coloured three-to-five-lobed leaves, tall upright growth. Good, moist soil).

MALUS 'John Downie' and new Canadian varieties (glowingly coloured apples).

NYSSA SYLVATICA (colours best in full sun in damp ground or near waterside).

PARROTIA PERSICA (horizontally branched tree with beech-like leaves that start to colour to crimson and russet at the end of July).

SORBUS—Additional species should include the pinky-white-fruited DISCOLOR, bright red ESSERTEAUIANA, blush HUPEHENSIS and MATSUMURANA (brilliant in both leaf and berry).

## For Winter Blossom

PRUNUS SUBHIRTELLA AUTUMNALIS and P.S.A. 'Rosea' (clouds of white or soft pink blossom in November or later with bursts in following mild spells until March), P. DAVIDIANA ALBA (beautiful white, February-flowering peach for sheltered places).

# Additional Shrub Suggestions
# for the Wild Garden

### Spring-flowering Shrubs

CHAENOMELES (Cydonia) 'Knaphill Scarlet', 'Boule de Feu', 'Aurora', 'Rowallane Seedling' (shades of terra-cotta and blood-red), 'Nivalis' (white), 'Apple Blossom' (good free-standing bushes in grass or among heather, or may be grown against a quarry face).

CORYLOPSIS GLABRESCENS, PAUCIFLORA, SPICATA and VEITCHIANA (pretty shrubs for early spring. Primrose-scented, racemes of small flowers. Sheltered position. Not for frost pockets).

OSMANTHUS DELAVAYI (sweetly-scented shrub for April with daphne-like white flowers covering the dark-leafed evergreen bush. Small, neat, holly-like foliage. Full sun in North).
× OSMAREA BURKWOODII (similar to Osmanthus but more vigorous and tougher for cold districts).

PIERIS FLORIBUNDA, FORMOSA FORRESTII and JAPONICA (acid soil. Slim attractive evergreen foliage. Brilliant salmon or red young leaves. Fountains of creamy Lily-of-the-Valley flowers. Wind shelter. Not for frost pockets).

PRUNUS TENELLA GESSLERIANA (dwarf almond with fresh green leaves and small, bright pink starry flowers. Thicket forming. Pretty above muscari or blue primroses).

STACHYURUS PRAECOX (nut-like bush flowering February-March with stiffly pendant racemes of pale yellow flowers. Peat. Full sun).

## Shrubs for Early Summer

CEANOTHUS THYRSIFLORUS, RIGIDUS, 'Edinensis', 'A. T. Johnson' (for cliffs, quarries and sheltered sunny banks. Boulder over roots will prevent wind-rock).

CHOISYA TERNATA (glossy-leafed evergreen with scented white, heavy-textured orange-blossom flowers from May on. Not fully hardy in bleak districts).

EMBOTHRIUM COCCINEUM, LANCEOLATUM 'Norquinco Valley Form' (brilliant tomato-scarlet honeysuckle flowers against dark lanceolate, evergreen leaves. Tall slender bushes. Woodland. Wind shelter. Will not stand drought. West and South).

ENKIANTHUS CAMPANULATUS and CHINENSIS (acid soil. Deciduous. Small but attractive pendent bells of buff tinged pink. Fine autumn colour. Heathland or wood).

ERINACEA PUNGENS (Hedgehog Broom. Spring dwarf bush with blue-purple pea-flowers. Hot dry position).

LEUCOTHÖE CATESBAEI (acid soil. Evergreen leathery pointed leaves. Arching branches with pendent Lily-of-the-Valley flowers. Thicketing. Heath or wood).

ROSA PRIMULA (the Incense Rose with small potentilla-like flowers of butter yellow and incense-scented foliage), *R.* 'Canary Bird' (one of the finest May-flowering yellows with ferny foliage and very beautiful deep yellow single roses), R. WILLMOTTIAE (scented foliage and quite large rose-purple flowers).

STAPHYLEA HOLOCARPA ROSEA (pinnate-leafed shrub with dense rose-pink panicles of flower very freely borne. Not often obtainable but well worth seeking. Easily grown in any reasonable soil).

SYRINGA PERSICA, SWEGINZOWII and Preston hybrid lilacs of which 'Bellicent', 'Fountain' and 'Elinor' are among the best. More suitable for the wild garden than are the conventional hybrids.

TAMARIX TETRANDRA (feathery pink-flowered Tamarisk. Good on cliffs or near sea).

### *Mid-Summer-to-Late Blossom*

AESCULUS PARVIFLORA (shrubby, eight-foot Horse Chestnut with elegant panicles of pink-stemmed white Horse Chestnut flowers. Suckering habit. Full sun and good loam).

BUDDLEIA FALLOWIANA 'Loch Inch', B.F. ALBA and B. ALTERNIFOLIA (B. FALLOWIANA and its varieties are graceful, grey-leafed shrubs for sun with fragrant flowers in July and August. B. ALTERNIFOLIA has an elegant weeping habit and flowers in June. Good for poor soil).

CARYOPTERIS × CLANDONENSIS (feathery misty-blue dwarf shrub for sun and poor soil).

CEANOTHUS 'Gloire de Versailles' (deciduous) and C. 'Autumnal Blue' (evergreen. Both need full sun and wind shelter.)

CERATOSTIGMA WILLMOTTIANUM (another late 'blue'. Sky-blue flowers in close-packed heads. Two-foot mounds. Full sun).

CLERODENDRUM TRICHOTOMUM (white flowers with persistent red calyx which enhances the bright-blue berries. C. T. FARGESII is similar but has a green calyx. Full sun).

CLETHRA ALNIFOLIA and DELAVAYI (the Sweet Peppers. Very fragrant August shrubs with airy racemes of white flowers. C. DELAVAYI is bolder in flower with black centres. Peaty soil and sun or part shade. Good near water).

DEUTZIA CORYMBOSA (fragrant), SETCHUENENSIS CORYMBIFLORA and 'Magician' (useful July shrubs as they will stand full shade, will do in poor soil and are attractive in flower).

DIPELTA FLORIBUNDA (tall June-flowering relation of the weigelas with pink, yellow-throated foxglove flowers. Sun. Any soil).

FABIANA VIOLACEA (milder districts only but most attractive for a sheltered sunny bank or to grow against a rock face with heath-like foliage and conspicuous tubular flowers of misty mauve-blue).

HIBISCUS SYRIACUS (full sun. Useful for late colour with large hollyhock flowers in blue, rose-red, white or pink. 'Coeleste' (blue), 'Woodbridge' (rose) and 'Snowdrift' are particularly good varieties).

HOHERIA LYALLII (one of the loveliest tall flowering shrubs for July with cool, shapely, glabrous leaves and clusters of white flowers like those of a cherry. Any good soil).

KOLKWITZIA AMABILIS (the Beauty Bush is a pretty June-flowering shrub for sun with feathery grey-green foliage and small pink foxglove flowers).

LEPTOSPERMUM SCOPARIUM and its varieties 'Nicholsii' in rosy crimson and 'Chapmanii'—pink. (Mild area shrub for full sun. Most attractive against a cliff or quarry face or will grow in open in really mild districts.)

MYRTUS COMMUNIS, M.C. TARENTINA, UGNI and LUMA (the Myrtles. For very mild areas only. M. LUMA has most attractive dappled bark and forms pleasing clumps in South-West).

OLEARIA MACRODONTA (useful shrub to break force of sea-wind. Grey holly-like leaves and white daisy flowers), O. SEMI-DENTATA (silver-felted, toothed leaves and lavender-purple daisy flowers with dark-purple centres. Lovely but for mild seaside areas only).

PHILADELPHUS species and hybrids (the Mock-Orange Blossoms of which DELAVAYI, 'Beauclerk', 'Belle Etoile', 'Sybille' and 'Voie Lactée' are perhaps the best for the wild garden).

TAMARIX PENTANDRA (rose-pink flowers in August and September).

VIBURNUM PLICATUM var. TOMENTOSUM 'Mariesii' and 'Lenarth' (midsummer flowering. Horizontal branches and flat, handsome lace-cap flowers of white against fresh green leaves. Shrub of great quality for orchard, woodland or grass).

WEIGELA (coarse-leafed but useful summer-flowering shrubs for grass with foxglove flowers in pink, white or yellow).

## Shrubs for Autumn Colour

CALLICARPA BODINIERI GIRALDII (GIRALDIANA) (violet-purple berries in large bunches. Leaves purple-tinted in autumn. Grouped plants—three to four in a group—fruits best. Full sun. Good loamy soil).

COTINUS AMERICANUS (RHUS COTINOIDES), C. COGGYGRIA (RHUS COTINUS), and 'Notcutt's Variety' (colour well).

DISANTHUS CERCIDIFOLIUS (fine autumn colours of claret, crimson and orange. Heart-shaped leaves like those of the Judas Tree. Hardy but should have wind shelter to preserve leaves).

EUONYMUS SPECIES (spindle-berries—all are good but fruit better where several are grown in proximity. E. ALATUS, PLANIPES, HAMILTONIANUS, YEDOENSIS and EUROPAEUS and its varieties are my favourites).

FOTHERGILLA MONTICOLA (fluffy white flowers in May and brilliant autumn foliage. Part shade. Acid soil).

OSMANTHUS HETEROPHYLLUS (ILICIFOLIUS) 'Purpureus' (small neat holly-leaves. Purple young foliage. Scented flowers in autumn).

## Winter-Blooming Shrubs

CORNUS MAS (puffs of small yellow flowers in February. Very hardy and bright if planted where the winter sunlight will catch it).

DAPHNE LAUREOLA (the wild green daphne of limestone woodland) and D. MEZEREUM (rose-purple) and its white variety ALBA. Semi-shade. Cool soil).

GARRYA ELLIPTICA (lovely for bank or top of rock face down which its long ropes of grey-green, rose-flushed suedey catkins can droop. Evergreen dark foliage).

PRUNUS INCISA PRAECOX (Cloudy blush pink, February-flowering bush cherry).

PRUNUS MUME (February-March-blooming apricot in varieties for warm, sheltered places).

# Recommended Reading

NOTE: Some of these books are out of print, but could be borrowed via the Regional Libraries Scheme of the Public Libraries and by Fellows from the R.H.S. Library.

*A Woodland Garden*, *A Garden in Wales* and *The Mill Garden* by A. T. Johnson (*Country Life*).

*My Garden in Spring, Summer and Autumn and Winter* by E. A. Bowles (three volumes) (Jack).

*Wood and Garden* and *Wall and Water* by Gertrude Jekyll.

*Berried Treasure* by Frank Kingdon Ward.

*The Native Garden* and *The Tranquil Gardener* by Robert Gathorne-Hardy (Nelson).

*Colour In The Winter Garden* and *Modern Shrub Roses* by Graham Thomas (Phoenix).

*Hardy Bulbs I and II* and *Herbaceous Plants* (Joint Handbooks Penguin Books and R.H.S.).

*Gardening In The Shade* by Margery Fish (Collingridge).

*A Flower For Every Day* by Margery Fish (Vista).

*The Savill Gardens in Windsor Great Park* by Lanning Roper.

*Seaside Gardening* by Christine Kelway (Collingridge).

*The Heather Garden* by F. J. Chapple (Collingridge).

*The Daffodil* by M. J. Jefferson-Brown (Faber).

*Gardening on Sand* by Christine Kelway (Collingridge)

*The Oxford Book of Birds* by B. Campbell and D. Watson (Oxford University Press)

## Useful Addresses

### Recommended Suppliers of Trees and Shrubs and Shrub Roses
### (including Rhododendrons, Azaleas)

Messrs. HILLIER & SONS, Nurserymen,
Winchester, Hants.

Messrs. HYDON NURSERIES,
Hydon Heath, Godalming, Surrey.

Messrs. KNAPHILL NURSERIES,
Lower Knaphill, Nr. Woking, Surrey.

Messrs. R. C. NOTCUTT,
Woodbridge, Suffolk.

Messrs. JAMES SMITH & SONS,
Darley Dale, Derbyshire.

Messrs. SUNNINGDALE NURSERIES
Windlesham, Surrey.

The MAGNOLIA GARDENS
Westmarsh, Surrey.

### Herbaceous Plants. Ground Cover

Capt. RALPH ALDERSEY (also some shrubs),
Aldersey Gardens, Aldersey, Nr. Chester.

Mrs. MARGERY FISH,
East Lambrook Manor, South Petherton, Somerset.

Messrs. REGINALD KAYE (also Water Plants and some Shrubs),
Waithman Nurseries, Silverdale, Lancashire.

Messrs. PERRY'S HARDY PLANT NURSERIES (also Water
Plants and Hardy Orchids),
Enfield, Middlesex.

Messrs. SUNNINGDALE NURSERIES (Shrubs and Rhododendron
        specialists also
Windlesham, Surrey.

## Uncommon Seeds

Messrs. THOMPSON & MORGAN, Seedsmen,
Ipswich.

## Bulbs

Messrs. WALTER BLOM,
Leavesden, Nr. Watford, Hertfordshire.

J. A. MARS, Esquire (Uncommon species),
Derreen, Bell Vale, Haslemere, Surrey.

Messrs. HYDE SNOWDROPS,
Hyde, Chalford, Gloucestershire.

# Index

188